BROTHER ANDREW

God's Undercover Agent

D1052133

Alan Millwright

BARBOUR
PUBLISHING, INC.
Uhrichsville, Ohio

Other books in the "Heroes of the Faith" series:

Gladys Aylward

William and Catherine Booth

John Bunyan

William Carey

Amy Carmichael

George Washington Carver

Fanny Crosby

Frederick Douglass

Jonathan Edwards

Jim Elliot

Charles Finney

Billy Graham

C. S. Lewis

Eric Liddell

David Livingstone

Martin Luther

D. L. Moody

Samuel Morris

George Müller

Watchman Nee

John Newton

Florence Nightingale

Mary Slessor

Charles Spurgeon

Hudson Taylor

Corrie ten Boom

Mother Teresa

Sojourner Truth

John Wesley

Scripture quotations are taken from the Authorized King James Version of the Bible.

Published by Barbour Publishing, Inc., P.O. Box 719, Uhrichsville, OH 44683
http://www.barbourbooks.com

Cover illustration © Dick Bobnick.

Member of the
Evangelical Christian
Publishers Association

Printed in the United States of America.

BROTHER
ANDREW

one

Eight-year-old Andy van der Bijl had quite a reputation. In December 1936, in his Dutch village of Sint Pancras, there wasn't anyone as reckless as he. At least Andy's parents didn't think so. As surely as winter brought freezing temperatures, Andy had to be the first to try the ice on the canal that paralleled the "dike road," which was the main street of Sint Pancras. An older person would have broken through the ice, but that didn't stop Andy. He had come to the conclusion that the villagers—especially the pious Whetstras—were too faint-hearted to try the ice.

"Aren't you afraid of falling through the ice?" queried Andy's friends anxiously.

"Of course I'm afraid," he replied slyly.

He knew real courage was doing something in spite of being afraid. That's why he said he was afraid even when he wasn't. Did that mean he was stupid not to be afraid? He didn't think he was stupid. Or could a boy be stupid in some things and smart in others?

His older brother Bastian was like that. "Bas" could not go to school because he seemed to be in another world: He could not carry on a conversation and he could not dress himself. Every day except the coldest days of January, Bas walked out of the house shortly after dawn and stationed himself under one of the elm trees that lined the dike road. It was always the same tree but not one by his family's yard. Standing all day long under an elm tree three houses away, he nodded at everyone who passed. Bas was now fourteen years old, and the only words he could say— "Aaaah, Bas"—were the sad ones everyone said to him.

Bas's handicap was hard for Andy to understand. Why would God allow such a tragedy? Andy wondered. The answer came to him as Bas revealed something that surpassed human understanding.

In the tiny parlor of the van der Bijl home, the smallest house in Sint Pancras, was a pump organ. Papa played hymns almost every evening, if he wasn't off repairing some damage Andy had caused that day. Papa's fingers were like rough, old cord wood from his years of plying his trade as a blacksmith. And because Papa was almost deaf, he didn't hear how he mangled the music. But despite his feeble efforts, everyone knew Papa was only warming up the organ—so that Bas could sit at his feet with his head pressed against the baseboard.

"See how dreamy Bas looks," gushed Geltje, Andy's younger sister. Geltje was still young enough to be awed by the miracle that took place in their small house. Invariably Bas would rise after several hymns and tap Papa on the shoulder. Then, never having seen how Papa's fingers had touched the keys or how Papa's fingers had pulled the knobs, Bas would play the very same hymns, but flawlessly! On summer nights villagers would gather outside and peer in the windows, tears streaming down their faces. Seeing Bas, Andy had a sense that God was in control, that this miracle was His plan. For how else could the dim-witted Bas do such a thing?

Yet the sense of God being in control somehow did not impart to Andy a desire to be good. If Mama had told him once she had told him a hundred times that the feast day for the real Sint Pancras was May 12, just one day after Andy's birthday. Somehow she hoped this coincidence—although no one seemed able to recall just what this Saint Pancras had done—would make him feel obligated to be saintly. Indeed, Mama thought Andy was about as unsaintly as a boy could be—and she didn't even know all the bad things he did.

His continuing masterpiece of mischief was his church "attendance" every Sunday. Papa always had to sit in the first pew because of his deafness. But because the family numbered eight with Andy's two sisters and three brothers, they never found enough room in the first pew. That worked out well for Andy, who made sure he straggled in late. No one thought much about Andy always withdrawing politely to another pew, even if it were the very back pew. But Andy made sure no one watched him as he slouched, slipped off the pew, crawled to the back door, and sneaked outside. In the dead of winter he amused himself by skating on the canal in his heavy wooden shoes. In summer he sat among lowing dairy cattle in pastures

7

beyond the canal. He breathed in rich scents coming from nearby fields flowering with hyacinths and tulips. On his back he watched gulls soar overhead. Even lying down he could be seen from any vantage point in Sint Pancras because its two churches and many houses were all built on mounds. But what was the danger with everyone but Andy in church at that hour?

Just before the service ended Andy would slip back to church and hang around the door by the pastor. Andy seemed to be greeting as many of the exiting people as the pastor. In fact, he was soaking up choice comments on the sermon. "Pastor, I loved your point about Psalm 120," one of the congregation would gush. Tiny bits of praise like that were all Andy needed. Then, after church, when the villagers gathered in homes to drink strong black coffee and the men to smoke cigars, everyone would discuss the sermon. This was Andy's opportunity to "prove" he had been in church during the sermon. He knew it was important to speak up first, long before the cigars were lit.

"Don't you think the pastor made a good point about Psalm 120?" he would scream to Papa. Of course by screaming at Papa, instead of addressing someone like Uncle Johan in a normal tone, Andy made sure everyone in the house heard his observation. No one could claim he had missed the service and that he only picked up the thread of the sermon by listening to the comments over coffee. He had never been caught in his deception yet—at least not outrightly. Later this day, however, his older sister Maartje did press him on Psalm 120. Was he supposed to know every psalm by heart? He listened impatiently as she quoted some verses of the psalm herself:

Deliver my soul, oh Lord,
from lying lips, and from a deceitful tongue.
What shall be given unto thee?
or what shall be done unto thee,
thou false tongue?

"Quite riveting," said Andy. "If only I could remember the next verse. . . ."

"Perhaps it would do you no good," snapped Maartje. "Some people have the whole Bible in their head but not one word of it in their heart."

"Perhaps," he agreed, too uninterested to catch her meaning.

People who quoted the Bible irritated Andy, and no one irritated Andy more than members of the Whetstra family. They were just trying to prove they were better than everyone. "God bless you, Andy," they would greet him. *Why don't we let God decide that,* fumed Andy silently. When they prefaced a remark with "if the Lord be willing," Andy didn't like that either. They were so self-righteous, so goody-goody. And they never seemed to get angry.

One day Andy had a chance to test their temper. He was walking down the dike road, passing every house in the village, since every house in the village was built next to the road, with a tiny bridge spanning a ditch. "What's this?" he murmured as he approached the Whetstra house. It was summer, but smoke was pluming from the chimney of the Whetstra house. Andy tiptoed across the tiny bridge and slipped behind their elm tree to observe. Seeing nothing, he left the tree to slip around the side of the house. There from behind a stand of daffodils he peered into the open kitchen window. Mrs. Whetstra was placing a tray of gingerbread cookies in the oven of her wood stove. What luck! He would wait until she removed the tray and brought the delicious cookies to the window to cool. Then I will find out just how righteous one of her gingerbread cookies is, he thought, giggling to himself.

But when he spotted a pane of glass leaning against the side of the house, his fertile brain hatched an even better plan. He would have to sacrifice his cookie, but it was too good a plan to ignore. He crept over and took the glass. Behind the house was the ladder that every villager in Sint Pancras kept by his house to climb up on the thatched roof. It seemed a thatched roof needed constant repair, not that Andy wanted to find out. Andy propped the ladder up and climbed onto the roof. There he gently placed the pane of glass over the smoking chimney. Quickly he descended and hid behind the daffodils. He could hardly keep from cackling with delight as smoke billowed from the stove and Mrs. Whetstra screamed, then began fanning the smoke away from her stove with her apron. He wanted to guffaw at the top of his lungs as Mr. Whetstra bolted from the house and gawked up at the chimney. "Now we'll hear some un-Christian cursing," Andy said, laughing. But Mr. Whetstra did no more than frown as he rushed behind the house to climb the ladder and remove the pane. Still, it was a delicious triumph to chew on.

Yet even that small triumph turned to sand in his mouth when Mr. and Mrs. Whetstra came to his house a few weeks later for coffee after the church service. Andy had screamed his usual clever remark at Papa so that everyone there, except possibly Maartje, would believe he had absorbed the sermon. Mr. Whetstra looked at Andy with a knowing look on his face. Had he seen Andy slip out of the church? He was just the sort of stuffed shirt who would spoil Andy's wonderful deception. He would tell the world about it! Andy felt sick as Mr. Whetstra approached him.

"You'll have to drop by our house and have a cookie, Andy," said Mr. Whetstra. "Our stove is working again, since I put in our new window pane."

Andy nodded and laughed weakly. So Mr. Whetstra knew. Papa would thrash him good for plugging Mr. Whetstra's chimney. Papa was tolerant with Andy's tricks around home, but he would not like Andy pulling tricks on neighbors. But Mr. Whetstra said no more.

Andy had quite a few skeletons in his closet. There weren't many people in Sint Pancras he hadn't victimized. Of course, his sisters and little brother Cornelius were easy pickings. But Andy even preyed on Ben, his brother, older by two years. Ben was an industrious fellow, tending gardens and doing odd jobs, and he had a fat piggy bank. The bank was so heavy he never missed the money Andy stole from it. That money bought Andy delicious poffertjes, or sugared fritters, at the small village bakery. Even his good friend Kees was not exempt from Andy's skulduggery. Once Andy broke his wooden shoe over his friend's head and Papa had to wire the shoe together again. "Now perhaps you can do that to Kees's head," said Andy, but not loud enough for Papa to hear.

Even Mama was not spared his larceny. Andy wouldn't think twice about slacking off on a chore she gave him, although her health was not good. Often she just sat in a chair and listened to religious programs on the radio. If Andy were supposed to weed the garden, he idly pawed at the weeds with a hoe. If he were supposed to do laundry on a washboard, he soon complained his arm hurt. Ben was always more than happy to show him up. If he were supposed to peel potatoes, his pitiful effort was so unappetizing he was soon relieved by one of his sisters. If he were supposed to get Papa's good leather shoes ready for church, it was just too easy to trick Cornelius into polishing them. "They shine like mirrors," Andy would say, admiring his own thin, mischievous face in the reflection. "No one has ever polished them that well before, Cornelius."

The only person Andy never intentionally took advantage of was Bas. As crass as Andy was, he would have been crushed by feelings of guilt, especially after Bas became very sick with tuberculosis. Hour after hour he coughed. The hacking went through Andy like thrusts of a knife. Then Bas became so sick Mama and Papa gave him their own bedroom. Soon Bas could no longer get out of bed. His coughs became weaker and weaker. The other children were not allowed to see him, for tuberculosis is highly contagious. The day after his eleventh birthday, Andy could no longer stand not seeing Bas. He slipped into the bedroom. Bas was so thin and white he looked like a corpse! Andy began crying. He kissed Bas again and again before he left. The world no longer seemed fun for Andy. Why was God so mean to Bas?

Two months later, at age seventeen, Bas died. It was July 1939.

"It may have been a blessing," said Mr. Whetstra. "He died in a house full of love. The Germans would have killed him. He would have been of no use in their utopia."

Andy was so tired of Mr. Whetstra's harangues about the Germans. Yes, Andy had heard Germany was controlled by a political party called the National Socialist German Workers. Some called its Socialist members "Nazis." The Nazis deemed all the elderly, feeble-minded, and physically handicapped as enemies of progress. Jews were added as enemies, too, then the Communists. The Nazis were led by a dictator named Adolf Hitler. To Andy, he appeared pompous and laughable, even comical. But Mr. Whetstra kept telling everyone there was nothing amusing about him at all.

Most of the villagers, including Andy's poor family, had radios, and occasionally while pursuing a pleasant music concert they would accidentally tune in a station that shrieked threats that seemed straight from hell. The screaming devil was Hitler! After that he was not comical, even to Andy.

Hitler soon showed he was not just a screamer when the Germans took the country of Czechoslovakia simply by making threats. Then an event took place in late 1939 that chilled Mr. Whetstra.

"Germany just signed a peace treaty with Russia," he said in a somber voice. "Hitler just made the Russians spectators in what will follow."

"And what is that?" demanded a nervous voice.

"Next the Nazis will take Poland just as Hitler said they would!"

One week later Germany armies assailed Poland in what Hitler bragged was his blitzkrieg or "lightning war." The Poles fought hard, but the battle was too lopsided. Hitler's tanks crushed men and horses of the Polish cavalry.

Just as Hitler said, his blitzkrieg was sudden and devastating. When the Germans split Poland with Russia, everyone knew why the Russians agreed to stay out of the conflict. Next the Americans declared their neutrality. But the French and British, both of whom had treaties with Poland, declared war on Germany. Nothing more happened for several weeks. Then the Russians invaded Finland.

One evening someone said, "Holland was neutral in the Great War. We will be neutral in this one, too."

Mr. Whetstra spoke reluctantly. "The devil Hitler may not permit any country to stay neutral in this one."

Suddenly, in April 1940, Germany invaded Norway and Denmark. Hitler said he had to protect them from the French and the British. Finally, Holland mobilized. To slow any German invasion, Holland did something that broke every Dutchman's heart: They began to flood lands that they had, over many hundreds of years, rescued from the sea, lands known as polders. The 1930s had been especially prosperous for Holland. The decade began with the reclamation of a huge polder just northeast of Sint Pancras called Wieringermeer Polder. That was followed by completion of a nearly twenty-mile dike separating the great inland Zuider Zee from the Wadden Zee.

"Now we are flooding the polders!" lamented Papa.

The flooding was supposed to slow down the Germans if they invaded. What it did was cause thousands of Dutch who farmed the polderlands to become refugees, and many were to be found in Sint Pancras. But they would not go hungry, for Holland's surplus supply of milk, cheese, and vegetables—all exports—now was put to good use. The pots in Sint Pancras seldom stopped bubbling rich split-pea soup or hutspot, a stew of vegetables and bacon, in an effort to feed these victims of the war.

On May 10, 1940, the Prime Minister of Holland reassured the Dutch by radio that Holland was neutral. That very night the southern sky erupted in lightning and thunder. Deadly noises wafted in the night air.

"That is not a thunderstorm!" screamed someone in the night.

It was war!

Andy's heart was racing. War! What did it mean? Surely the heroic Dutch would beat back the stupid Germans. Andy and his family rushed to the radio. The news was terrifying: The Germans were bombing airports all over Holland. German soldiers had parachuted into Moerdijk, Rotterdam, and Dordrecht. The Germans wanted to capture bridges in those three critical places, speculated the announcer, so their tanks could move freely back and forth from northern Holland to southern Holland.

The next dawn the villagers strolled the dike road in a daze. It was May 11. No one remembered until later that it was Andy's twelfth birthday, not even Andy! Then aircraft flew overhead from the east. German planes! Bombs exploded nearby. There was a military airfield between Sint Pancras and the large town of Alkmaar five miles to the south. "Get back inside," yelled Papa, who could hear well enough the booms of war.

The Dutch people could do little else but wait. Queen Wilhelmina fled to Britain on May 13, while Princess Juliana and her toddling daughter Beatrix escaped to Canada. The valiant Dutch army imploded into a small area from Amsterdam to Rotterdam that they dubbed "Fortress

Holland," as if such a move made them impregnable against the Nazi blitzkrieg. Two days later Fortress Holland surrendered. The 18th Army of German Army Group B under General Fedor von Bock goose-stepped into Amsterdam in crisp gray and black uniforms. Parading with them were tanks and cannons and trucks and half-tracks and hundreds of huge red flags, each with a black swastika inside a white circle. The voices on the radio now spoke Dutch with a German accent. The Dutch were assured that the Germans were there only to defend them against the French and British aggressors. "This war seems destined to be so monstrous it is already being called World War II!" lamented villagers.

Even Sint Pancras soon had its contingent of Germans. The arrival of any automobile in the village was cause for gawking. But one day an automobile bearing ominous swastikas rolled up in front of the mayor's house. A portly German lieutenant got out and quickly commandeered the house. He and his platoon would use the mayor's residence as their personal quarters.

But to one very observant boy, the conquerors of Sint Pancras could hardly be considered crack troops. Andy van der Bijl was about to wage his own war against Germany.

two

A s the occupation of Sint Pancras by the Germans began, Hitler deemed all of Holland now part of the glorious Third Reich. His Nazi utopia, he bragged, was going to be the third great reich, or empire, after the Holy Roman Empire (regarded as the first German empire) and the German Empire (1871–1919). The Third Reich would rule for a thousand years, he boasted.

At first the occupation did not seem so evil. It just seemed as if the Germans, who had a genius for organizing, were making life more efficient. All Dutch citizens had to carry an identity card in a pouch hanging from a necklace. Food and merchandise had to be purchased with coupons from ration books.

"Is it so bad to be organized?" some Dutch people asked.

Mr. Whetstra cautioned, "Don't be fooled. This just means the Nazis are more patient than we realized."

A nightly curfew of ten o'clock was met with little

resistance from the Dutch. "What respectable citizen would be out in the streets then anyway?" reasoned some villagers. Soon no Dutch could have a telephone, but that did not affect Andy's poor family. Then came media censorship: The Dutch newspapers no longer carried any real news. The real news that the Dutch heard over radio broadcasts from Britain was depressing anyway.

"All of Europe is being 'organized' into the Third Reich," grumbled some cynical villagers. "Who wants to read the news?"

But when the villagers were commanded to turn in their radios they were upset. The Dutch loved to listen to their music concerts. Andy's mother especially liked religious broadcasts from Hilversum. As law abiding as Mama was, even she considered hiding their radio. When the family chose to hide the radio in a crawl space in the loft, Mama wasn't happy with that, but she realized that anywhere in the main part of the house was too risky. To get the news each night, one small member of the family slipped into the crawl space to listen. Then the listener reported the news to the rest of the family.

"The Germans have all of France," reported one listener in early June 1940. "They pushed the British army right off the European continent at a place called Dunkirk."

New Nazi restrictions continued to grow like cancers, as Papa soon realized when his modest mode of transportation was hindered. He owned a bicycle that he pedaled into Alkmaar for his job. German soldiers were now stopping riders and confiscating the rubber tires. A practical people, most Dutch shrugged, knowing that rubber was precious to the Nazis now that the supply was all in the hands of their enemies. Papa shrugged, too. Like the others, he soon wrapped the rims with cloth and rode his bicycle anyway.

But one day he came home walking. "The soldiers took my bicycle," he said dejectedly.

"Rubber!" snorted Mr. Whetstra. "Now we know the Nazis don't want the Dutch people moving around."

As time went on, the Nazis moved the nightly curfew earlier and earlier. Soon all Dutch citizens were forbidden to be out after dark. To the Nazis, after dark was an opportune time for Dutch "troublemakers" to move around. But one of the most disturbing developments came shortly thereafter. German soldiers not only used the schoolhouse for a barracks, but the teacher, Miss Meekle, was dismissed. Schooling for all ages ended, and no one knew when classes would begin again. "Perhaps when the Nazis install their own teachers," more than one villager offered. Certainly the Nazis could not trust the Dutch teachers in the schools who, they asserted, had such "old-fashioned" ideas. So Andy's education was over for a while. He had completed the sixth grade. Since Andy didn't like studying, he was not brokenhearted about school being closed. But some of his older friends actually gave him a good reason to prefer no school.

"Perhaps it is good to have no school now, Andy," reasoned his older friends. "That way you can nap during the day so you are rested for the night."

"I see!" gushed Andy. "This time the Nazis really have been stupid."

Andy had heard there was an "Underground" of Dutch resistance fighters. Members of the Underground were not about to trust a boy of thirteen, but maybe after he had proved himself a few times they would give him things to do. For a while he did not nap during the day. He was too busy scheming. He knew many Dutch worked around the obnoxious ration cards by trading goods with one another. So, one of the first things he did was to pick some tomatoes and cabbages to take into Alkmaar. "Perhaps I can trade these for something a little hotter," he said with a laugh.

In Alkmaar Andy intended to learn who might still be selling fireworks. But he learned some other things, too. He learned that the Nazis had double-crossed the Russians. Since June 1941, they had been fighting Russian troops on a battlefront east of Germany. That seemed a good thing to Andy. Wouldn't it mean the Nazis could devote less time to Holland? Then in Alkmaar he saw evil the likes of which he had never seen in his life. Signs were posted in some shops that read NO JEWS SERVED HERE. Surely those were just a few evil shopowners, he thought. But then he saw a sign in a public park: NO JEWS ALLOWED. "How can this be?" he gasped.

Such evil made him all the more determined to pester the Nazis. Soon he traded his vegetables for some run-of-the-mill firecrackers and one cherry bomb. That night at home Andy slipped down from the loft where he slept with his brothers. He left the house on barefoot. This would be no night for clomping around in wooden shoes.

No sooner had he left than he had to dive behind the house because German soldiers, betrayed by a flashlight one of them waved into the darkness, were coming up the road. After they passed, Andy dashed down the road in the opposite direction.

"I wish to serenade the good German lieutenant," he

announced quietly as he stood at the door of the mayor's house.

Suddenly he heard noises behind him. Light swept the front of the house. The patrol! Andy ducked down. But he was not going to stop now. He lit the fuse.

"Wer ist da?" screamed a voice in German.

"It's just me, the troubadour," Andy muttered as he threw the cherry bomb inside the lieutenant's window.

The cherry bomb probably saved him, for the patrol was diverted by the explosion. They had to make sure their lieutenant was all right. Meanwhile, Andy hid in a garden nearby. Never idle, he crawled around, feeling various plants. Finally his fingers played over fernlike leaves. Yes, the gardener still had some carrots unpicked. Andy pulled one, brushed off the dirt, and munched it contentedly as the patrol jabbered on the dike road.

A few days later he saw Mr. Whetstra. "There are signs in Alkmaar saying no Jews can shop in certain stores," he explained.

Mr. Whetstra sighed. "I've heard that all Jews will soon be required to sew a large yellow Star of David right on their clothing. Inside the star will be the word *Jood.*" *Jood* is the Dutch word for Jew.

Now each night Andy heard the roar of engines overhead. British radio said the Nazis were using Dutch airports to launch their bombing raids on Britain. One night in that summer of 1941, the sky to the south flickered with light. There was a great air battle above Holland. British planes were attacking German planes. The battle inflamed Andy. He had to step up his own attacks on the Germans. If he could prove himself, perhaps the Underground would use him.

One of the things that aggravated Andy most was the German lieutenant's automobile. The Dutch weren't even allowed to own bicycles. So Andy decided to even the score. This would require a cup of sugar.

"The lieutenant's automobile sure is running rough these days," commented Andy in mock sympathy to Mr. Whetstra a few days later. "Look at that plume of nasty black smoke from the exhaust pipe."

"Yes, I heard his spark plugs are very badly fouled, the sort of trouble that could be caused by sugar in the gas tank."

"But wouldn't putting sugar in a gas tank be against the laws of the Third Reich?" Andy asked with a smirk.

By November 1941 there was nothing funny about the Nazis to the Dutch. It was common knowledge now that Jews were being rounded up and sent to concentration camps. Dutch resistance fighters were being executed. Young Dutchmen were being sent to Germany to work in factories. Consequently, Jews and young Dutchmen began disappearing, literally "diving out of sight." Among these Onderduikers was Andy's seventeen-year-old brother Ben. All Andy knew was that Ben, one of the first to "disappear," was probably working on a farm somewhere in Holland. It was best not to know. The Nazi secret police, called the Gestapo, were already well known for using torture to pry secrets from people.

If a stranger appeared at the house, no one asked questions. If it were a woman it was probable she was a Jew, perhaps on her way to the coast just five miles west where she could escape Holland by boat. Across the North Sea was safety in Britain. Or perhaps she would hide in some household as a servant or "relative." If the stranger were a man, the possibilities were many. He might be a Jew, trying to escape Holland or perhaps hide on a farm. He might be an British airman who had been shot down. He might be one of the Dutch Underground in hiding. He might be one of the Onderduikers. "Life in Holland is a nightmare now," sighed Mama.

Some houses were adopted by the Dutch Underground as central hiding places for refugees. A team of craftsmen would come into the house and build a hiding place so cleverly hidden even bloodthirsty weasels like the Gestapo could not find it. But the small, simple cottage of Andy's family was certainly no candidate for a refuge. Still, Andy continued to try to prove himself to the Underground. Firecrackers and even sugar in the gas tank seemed like kids' pranks. So he began to steal from the Germans. There were many things he could steal that the Underground could use, such as bicycles and ration cards. But nothing was so dangerous to steal as a weapon.

The very feel of a two-pound Luger pistol, with its checkered walnut handle and blue barrel, was like death in Andy's hand. But steal it from a German officer's quarters he did, as well as a deadly little nine-ounce Walther "Vest Pocket" pistol! Stealing one of the Germans' many Mauser rifles was an easier task, but concealing a rifle was another story. If Andy were caught, any one of these weapons would be turned on him. By now he had no illusions about Nazis. They were killers. No, the fat lieutenant didn't seem the murderous type. But the lieutenant would murder if his own life depended on it. And his life did depend on it. "That is the way the godless Nazis enforce order," commented Mr. Whetstra.

23

Andy's contributions to the Underground finally won him a coveted position with the organization. His first assignment was to deliver verbal messages from one group to another, a job that depended on his skill as a runner. He had indeed become a fleet runner, and quite by accident. There were no great Dutch runners to inspire him, none that he had heard of in Sint Pancras anyway. In fact, he thought all great distance runners came from Finland, with the greatest of all being the Olympian Paavo Nurmi. But international competitive running was at a standstill thanks to the Nazis. Not even the Olympic games were held during these grim days.

As much as Andy would have liked to race, and as much as it might have been his redemption with the villagers who regarded him a rascal, there was no competitive running for him. Yet over the months and years he had conditioned himself to run mile after mile, barely tiring. It had nothing to do with a training program. Running did something to him. His legs churned as flawlessly as the blades of the great windmills that pumped water from the polders. After a few minutes of skimming barefoot across the polders and along the dike roads, Andy was warmed, then uplifted, with a feeling of bliss. His thoughts were more precise and more confident than at any other time. So very often he ran to overcome a feeling of hopelessness. And what began as happy jogs of six-minute miles became ecstatic lopes of five miles, then ten miles. Some of his runs lasted almost two hours!

If he had been religious, he would have praised God for this gift. But he was not religious, even though he believed in God. War just seemed to prove to him God was indifferent to suffering. Andy had thought that way since Bas, whom he considered the most innocent person alive, had suffered so terribly before dying. No, as far as Andy could determine even in his clearest moments, he had this gift of running for no apparent purpose whatever. The fact that he could deliver messages like a human greyhound for the Underground in a vicious war was a mere coincidence, but, he admitted, a lucky one.

After Andy proved himself to the Underground by delivering verbal messages, the powers that be allowed him to deliver written messages. Of course, to deliver the written message was much riskier. If Andy were caught by the Nazis, he could not lie his way out of trouble. He was even assigned to deliver an Underground newsletter to various groups. And the news by January 1943 was getting better. The tide had turned against Hitler. The Russians had stopped the advance of the German army in the east and were even thought to be pushing them back! At long last the sleeping giant, America, led by President Franklin Delano Roosevelt, had joined the fight.

"I wondered when that stubborn Dutchman Roosevelt was going to bring America into the fight," joked many in Holland, knowing Roosevelt was of Dutch descent.

The British and American armies routed crack German armies in North Africa. Germany's North African armies under Field Marshall Rommel had been considered invincible. Not now. Hitler would get no help from his Japanese allies either. They were being clobbered by the Americans in the Pacific. At last there seemed hope for Holland. Unfortunately, that winter in Holland was the worst in anyone's memory. Many people froze or starved to death. Food and fuel were in short supply. The villagers had to burn their elm trees that winter to survive.

And what a terrible time for the razzias, the Nazi man-power raids! A truck would careen into a village and unload a squad of soldiers to round up all older boys and young men. Rumor had it they were driven straight to Germany and worked to death in the factories, and no one doubted the rumors. At least no one had ever come back.

Only fourteen, Andy had to flee during these raids, too. He couldn't be sure an overzealous soldier wouldn't include him. But usually there was an advance warning of several minutes. Of all who fled he needed the least warn-ing time. Like all the others he would dash out across the fields. In a few minutes Andy was far ahead of the pack. Their sanctuary was a swamp beyond a high embankment built for a railway. There he and others hid among the reeds. The regular German soldiers were not dedicated devils like the Gestapo. There was little chance they would ever figure out that a swamp lay beyond the railway embankment. This flight seemed quite a lark for Andy in the summer, but in the winter it was hardly that. Until the swamp iced over, the refugees had to wait in the teeth-chattering cold water.

"Even an ornery rascal like Andy will not survive very many of those bone-numbing flights," whispered some villagers.

Before 1943 Andy could not remember the villagers not having plenty of food. But 1943 marked the end of those bountiful days. Papa even dug up the tulip bulbs, and the family ate them like potatoes. The polders had disappeared first. Then all the young men. Then the elms. Then the kip-pers, herrings, eels, rich soups and stews, Edam cheeses, sausages, cabbages, and potatoes. Now the tulips. It seemed that the Nazis were robbing the Dutch of everything that made them Dutch. The good news that the Germans finally appeared to be losing the war seemed a bitter irony.

"If everything Dutch is dead by the time the Germans surrender, what good will that do us?" wondered some villagers.

Yet they struggled grimly on. Andy stole food now. One food wholesaler he pilfered at night. With a pocket knife he patiently sliced off pieces of apple through the slats of the apple crates. Just one or two apples were not missed from a crate. To Andy his gnawing hunger justified stealing. But he became so used to stealing he stole at every opportunity. He told himself anything stolen might be useful to the Underground. So any item, no matter how seemingly irrelevant, was fair game from a Nazi or a Dutch citizen, in a shop or anywhere else. Cigarette lighters, pocket knives, and pencils were all part of his loot.

Month after month the Dutch people waited for the rumored invasion of Europe by the Americans and the British. They also heard rumors that Hitler had concentrated German armies on the northwest coast of France to prevent an invasion. There he put his best general in charge: Field Marshall Rommel. About this time Andy found himself in Alkmaar, in trade school. The Nazis did not like to see boys of Andy's age idle. He may have been too young to work in factories, but he could be prepared. By German order, he was commanded to become a machinist.

"Unless you want to serve the Third Reich as a mule you youngsters must learn something," barked the instructor.

Whether Andy liked it or not, he was introduced to the

tools machinists used to make metal parts: lathe, shaper, planer, and the milling machine. Eventually he might also learn how to use grinders, saws, and drills, he was told. If a student were particularly skilled, he might become an operator of the milling machine.

"The milling machine is the most versatile of all machine tools," said the instructor proudly.

Silently Andy wondered if that were a machine that could be used to make guns, guns to fight the Nazis.

Despite his interest in weaponry, Andy was not a good student. He had no desire to serve the Third Reich, even as one of their most skilled machinists. Instead of focusing on a skill, he daydreamed of a great invasion. Thousands of ships, thousands of planes, millions of soldiers. Summer came, then another dread winter. It was not until the summer of 1944 when Andy was sixteen that the invasion actually occurred. At last, the Allies had landed their forces at Normandy on the north coast of France, and Hitler's Nazis could not dislodge them.

Hitler's Third Reich was truly unraveling. In July 1944 several Germans tried to kill Hitler by setting off a bomb in a conference room. But their plan misfired as Hitler survived and four of his officers died. The war dragged on; by August the Allies had taken back Paris. And they clearly had superiority in the skies. Thousands of glittering planes now passed over Holland on the way to bomb Germany. In December the Nazis launched a surprise counterattack, called the Battle of the Bulge. It almost overwhelmed the Allies. But all the Dutch breathed gratefully when the German counterattack ultimately failed. Now it seemed everyone in Holland began to speculate on the endgame in this colossal war.

Some said, "The British and Americans have captured Brussels, so Belgium is almost free again. Holland will soon be free!"

But others countered, "Think about it. Yes, they have Brussels but they are going to bypass Holland and thrust their might straight into the evil heart of Germany!"

"No! Our good friends are going to free Holland first. . . ."

Then the speculation would take another turn. "Well, we know the Allies will get to Holland eventually. But what will the Nazis do then?"

"Surely they will be kind to us. That way we might forget their terrible crimes against us."

"But they could do just the opposite: exterminate everyone who ever gave them trouble. Dead men don't talk. . . ."

And so the speculation went on.

By February 1945 the Nazis had been in Holland almost five years. Anyone in the Underground had to restrain his elation over the impending German defeat. It was too soon to celebrate, but not too late to be executed by the Nazis: The Allied armies had indeed brushed past the bulk of Holland. The great American and British armies were positioned all along the border of Germany, from Holland south of the Maas River through Belgium and Luxembourg and France. The Germans in Sint Pancras talked about the war, too. They were every bit as interested in the war news as the Dutch. They listened to news broadcasts from Britain. They had given up listening to their own German radio broadcasts.

"The Nazi authorities always lie," grumbled the German soldiers.

On May 1, 1945, the radio brought the news that Hitler was dead. On May 5 his successor, Grand Admiral Doenitz, ordered the end of all resistance in northwest Germany, Denmark, and Holland. At last World War II was over for Holland.

Holland's liberation seemed almost anticlimactic. Suddenly all the Nazis were gone. The streets of Amsterdam were full of soldiers from the Canadian First Army. Ben returned from hiding on a remote farm. Naturally, Mr. Whetstra spoke of forgiveness despite the horrors of the Nazis. Yet there were people in Holland the Dutch hated even more than the Nazis. Those were the traitors, the Dutch who had helped the Nazis, the collaborators. After the Nazis left many collaborators were murdered and the rest were brought to trial. A guilty verdict was usually accompanied by a death sentence. It was a time of reckoning for many in Holland, but somehow Andy never expected his day of reckoning would come, too.

"Andy, Papa wants to see you," said Geltje one day when Andy returned home from a day of loitering around the village with the other older boys. "He's in the backyard."

"Hoeing the weeds that I was supposed to hoe, I suppose," grumbled Andy.

Papa was indeed hoeing weeds that threatened his fat cabbages. Andy took a deep breath and walked around in front of Papa. Papa was hoeing too intently to notice Andy.

"Did you want to see me, Papa?" screamed Andy.

Papa looked up. He wasn't smiling. "What are you going to do with your life?" he roared.

"I haven't decided," shouted Andy, sure that all the neighbors were now listening.

"What about becoming a blacksmith like me?" screamed Papa.

"I don't think so," shrieked Andy.

"Well, what about the trade of machine tooling?"

"It reminds me of the Nazis!" howled Andy.

All these verbal exchanges were delivered as loud as cannon blasts because of Papa's disability. But the only one that felt like a true cannon blast was Papa's last remark.

"You have until this fall to decide on a trade, Andy!" blared Papa.

Andy was being thrown out of the house!

three

A ndy's mind was reeling. What am I going to do? he thought hopelessly.

While the war was on, he had a purpose. Now he was bewildered. He had turned seventeen years old just the week after the war ended. Virtually robbed of his boyhood, he had no education past the sixth grade. During the war he had always thought of his refugee brother Ben as the one robbed of his future. But now Andy realized Ben had four years of schooling that he didn't have. Ben had ideas, plans, ambitions, even a steady girlfriend. Andy had none of those, and soon he would have no place to sleep and eat unless, that is, he picked a trade. "I must clear my head," he grunted as he ran across the tiny bridge to the dike road.

By the time he reached Alkmaar, five miles away, the cobwebs were gone. His mind was running as fast as his feet. He took stock of himself. He was uneducated, but he was a superb physical specimen. The extreme running had tempered much of his body into steely hardness. He was a machine that could run mile after mile, but there was little future in that. He was also skilled at stealing and lying. His work for the Underground had proved that. Suddenly he realized he was thinking too small. The Holland of 1945 was much more than the fifteen thousand square miles of water-sogged Netherlands hugging the North Sea. There was Dutch Guyana in South America, four times as big as the Netherlands. There was also a group of six small islands off South America called the Dutch West Indies. But the prize of Holland was a group of islands off Asia called the Dutch East Indies.

"Now the Dutch East Indies is truly enormous," marveled Andy, his mind becoming clearer and clearer.

The Dutch East Indies encompassed over thirteen thousand islands with a land area totaling nearly eight hundred thousand square miles—fifty times the size of the Netherlands! In fact, the Dutch East Indies was larger than Germany, France, Great Britain, and Holland combined. The island empire was no vast wasteland either. Thousands of people lived there. Andy knew now he was on to something. The Dutch had controlled this huge island empire for three hundred years. Only in this latest world war had they lost control of it temporarily. During the war the Japanese had conquered the Dutch East Indies, then armed and trained the natives there to help defend the islands. When the Japanese finally surrendered in August 1945, they encouraged the trained natives to rebel against the Dutch who were trying to reestablish control. Apparently Dutch soldiers still skirmished occasionally with these rebel natives.

Suddenly Andy's future was crystal clear. "I must be a

soldier!" he cried to no one in particular.

Mama and Mr. Whetstra were the only ones in Sint Pancras cool to Andy's idea. Mama came right out and asked Andy why he would want to kill anyone. Andy had not really thought about that. Kill someone? There was no actual war in the Dutch East Indies. Besides, he had seen real war. Most of the soldiers never killed anyone. They occupied villages. The ones in Sint Pancras just marched around and lived the good life. Although the soldiers were pestered, they usually bullied the natives whenever they felt like it. Why would it be any different for Andy in the Dutch East Indies? Why shouldn't I be stationed in some exotic South Pacific paradise? he asked himself.

Mr. Whetstra was sad to hear Andy wanted to be soldier. He just hoped Andy would find what he was looking for. No one questioned his desire to go to the Dutch East Indies. The island empire brought in a lot of money to Holland. The islands accounted for most of the world's quinine and pepper. They supplied enormous amounts of rubber, tea, tin, coffee, sugar, and oil, too. But the Dutch East Indies was not just a money cow. After three hundred years the Dutch were truly fond of these islands. Dutch homes displayed the colorful batik fabric, native Javan masks, Bali woodcarvings, peacock feathers, and pictures of jungled hillsides, all souvenirs of the islands.

"Paradise," said Andy confidently, the more he thought about it.

Andy borrowed Papa's bicycle and pedaled off to the nearest army recruiting office. But there Andy discovered he could not enlist in the army at all. He had to be eighteen. Even though Andy would not be eighteen until the next year, he didn't really mind waiting until May 11, 1946. The main thing was that Papa was satisfied he had picked a "trade." Meanwhile Andy would have an almost year-long vacation around Sint Pancras. When the village became insufferable he would run the dike roads as he usually did. Or from April until October he could stroll in to Alkmaar and watch the cheese market. He had forgotten during the lean war years how buyers plugged and grated the mounded lots of cheese, sniffing and tasting.

"Some say it is the finest cheese market in Holland," he would tell his friends.

His day to leave Sint Pancras finally came. After a tearful farewell from Mama, he eagerly left for basic training. Once there, he discovered he wasn't the perfect physical specimen he believed himself to be. Like all distance runners he was tightly muscled from his heels to his back of his neck. But his chest, abdomen, and quadriceps were little better than average. However, his instructors immediately singled him out as having great potential. They built up his chest, abdomen, and quadriceps, and they gave him special exercises to retain his flexibility. Soon Andy went though an obstacle course like no obstacles existed. Soon Andy was headed for Gorkum for special commando training. "I'm being trained for hand-to-hand fighting," Andy liked to tell any and all listeners.

In the army Andy was amazed to learn what had happened in the Dutch East Indies during World War II. In his mind, the Dutch sat out the war, accomplishing little more than throwing firecrackers at the Germans. In truth, while the Dutch in Holland sat out the war, the Dutch in the Pacific fought savagely against the Japanese. The war there was played out on a huge canvas. In January 1942 the enormous naval forces of Japan invaded the Dutch East Indies. The Japanese wanted the Dutch oil fields most of all. A naval force of four heavy cruisers and fifteen destroyers shelled the north end of the island of Borneo to soften it up for General Yamashita's foot soldiers. As the Japanese force proceeded south toward the great prize of the Indies, Java, Dutch aircraft attacked the ships.

"Dutch aircraft?" murmured an amazed Andy.

He was even more amazed to learn that Dutch Rear-Admiral Doorman attacked the Japanese naval forces with a fleet of his own. That the small Dutch force could not defeat the larger Japanese force did not bother Andy. What pleased him was to learn the Dutch had the courage and know-how to fight. Even Java finally falling into the hands of the Japanese did not bother him that much. The prize Dutch cruisers *Java* and *De Ruyter* fought until they were sunk. The Allies abandoned the islands to the Japanese, but the Dutch stayed and fought the foot soldiers of the Japanese 16th Army. "So we did fight on the sea, and in the air, and on the land," realized Andy with pleasure.

Still the opportunist, every Sunday while training, Andy would don his uniform and go to church. Often a young soldier would get invited to Sunday dinner, and Andy would never turn down a free meal. At these gatherings, he would be encouraged to eat heartily during dinner, and to smoke a cigar afterward (the Dutch were famous for their love of cigars). Usually by the time Andy left his host family he had recorded their name and address in his little notebook, with the promise he would write them from the Dutch East Indies. This he fully intended to do, in the hope some nice packages of treats would come to him in the return mail. If he were very lucky, the host family would have a pleasant daughter just about his age. That was how he met Thile, a beautiful girl he always thought of as Snow White because of her milky white skin and coal-black hair.

"Will there be fighting in the East Indies?" Thile wanted to know, breathlessly.

"Nothing I am not trained to handle," he answered breezily.

But truthfully he expected no trouble. Yes, the Japanese had trained some local natives as militia. But they were not well armed and they lacked unity. How could a backward villager in Java unite with a backward villager in Sumatra? Andy had learned that scholars thought there were forty-two racial types in the islands who spoke two hundred languages and practiced seven religions! If that were not enough disunity, the 13,667 islands of the empire stretched over a distance of 3,500 miles! Andy had heard that French troops had just started fighting the Vietnamese rebels in their colony Indochina, but that wasn't the Dutch East Indies. Why should he be concerned? When Andy left Holland in November 1946 aboard the Sibajak he expected to loaf in a tropical paradise. He was in a very good mood.

"Even Mama thrusting a Bible on me as I left home can't spoil my high spirits," he reflected on board ship.

The highest daily temperatures had been in the forties when he left Holland. Days were foggy with occasional light rain. By the time he reached the Dutch East Indies the temperatures had soared above any that he had ever experienced in Holland. Rain fell in buckets. The East Indies was in one of its two monsoon seasons, and Andy noticed his skin was never dry.

The capital of Java was the port city of Batavia. But that was a Dutch name, so the Japanese had renamed it Jakarta. Now it was known by both names. Certainly the city looked Dutch to Andy when he disembarked. The Dutch had built neat warehouses all along the wharf. Inland were the familiar Dutch canals. Houses had red-tile roofs. Pleasant squares were common. The Japanese, who had a fondness for order, had not changed the orderly Dutch touches. Even the Dutch governor-general's residence, the magnificent Merdeka Palace, was unscathed. It displayed fluted columns, a colonial facade, and chandeliers on its portico. Just as reassuring to Andy were the many red-brick homes, complete with steep tiled roofs, diamond-paned windows, and clock towers.

"Dutch all the way!" laughed one of the new soldiers in the open truck they were riding in.

But Andy soon discovered that there was another Batavia, perhaps several others. The Chinese inhabited the large area around the harbor known as Tanjung Priok. Pigtailed and pajamaed, they sold dry noodles and seaweed from tiny booths. Farther into the island Andy saw a profusion of betjaks in the street. These large, gaudily painted tricycles served as taxis. Away from the Dutch and Chinese sectors the streets narrowed and swarmed with pedestrians, betjaks, and carts drawn by lumbering buffaloes. The air was spicy with cinnamon, ginger, and cloves. Would Andy ever understand this part of Batavia? He didn't have a clue who these tan-skinned girls were in their ankle-length garments or what language they spoke. He recognized wares at a market they stopped at for a short time. Trays of powdered sandalwood and vanilla were among pyramids of pineapples, mangoes, papayas, bread-fruit, coffee beans, and garlic pods. They sold everything in the market from fabric and peanuts to pigs and cobras! These people might lack certain European luxuries but they were not poor.

Andy was especially intrigued by a monkey for sale. "That seems just the pet for this place!" he gushed, but an officer soon talked him out of it.

Near the edge of the city the countryside was heralded by vines of bougainvillea lining a rough dirt road. Here the betjaks were replaced by goats, chickens, and small children. Suddenly everything was lush and green! Now this is Java, thought Andy. It wasn't jungle but wide expanses of rice paddies. Small villages stood among the paddies like forested islands. Streams abounded, as did dense thickets of bamboo and groves of coco palms and bananas. Corn grew to maturity in just seven weeks. These people did not know hunger.

"This really is going to be paradise," sighed Andy.

Elected for special commando training, Andy joined an elite group on an island. There he learned about the natives of the East Indies from other commandos. The culture of the natives was far different from that of Holland. Most natives had little ambition for improving their lot, not because improvement was impossible but because improvement was not seen as particularly desirable. They ate well. They dressed as well as they wanted. It was easy enough to keep the rain off their heads. They got along with ambitious, meddlesome foreigners by any means available. Stealing and lying were always options. Andy found their attitude not that unusual.

"It is the way I dealt with the Germans," he reflected.

And yet there were natives of the East Indies with ambitions. Andy was surprised to learn rebel guerillas called PNI numbered about eighty thousand. Apparently, the Dutch forces in the East Indies were now about that same number. The PNI, led by a man named Sukarno, was in no way submissive. A real battle was brewing. But the vast superiority of Dutch weapons seemed of little use. Yes, they had modern tanks and cannons but the PNI would not fight European battles. They used hit and run guerilla tactics. Andy learned that a Communist named Musso was also organizing natives into guerilla units. Fortunately for the Dutch, the two native groups did not get along. But there would be plenty of skirmishes with both PNI and Communist guerillas.

"The perfect arena for Dutch commandos," concluded some of Andy's buddies.

On the island the new commandos trained in more hand to hand combat. They ran obstacle courses, swung over streams on vines, crawled belly-down through ditches, and fought with flailing hobnailed boots and hands stiffened into clubs. They fought with knives, too. Wiry Andy had extraordinary endurance. At the end of the day it was Andy who excelled. He became exceptionally confident, even for him. *Is there anything I can't do?* he wondered.

"Can you drive this Bren carrier?" An officer approached him one day.

"Yes, sir!"

"Drive it over to the motor pool for service!"

"Yes, sir!"

A Bren carrier was a large tanklike vehicle that transported men. It was on treads. Andy had never driven one but he had watched the drivers. It didn't seem so difficult. He turned the key and the engine started. His feet fumbled on the floorboard with the clutch and accelerator. The carrier lurched forward. But Andy could not locate the brake pedal and the carrier only stopped when it slammed into another carrier.

With the panache he had obtained from his encounters with German soldiers, Andy said in his sincerest voice, "I believe there's something wrong with the brakes, sir."

The red-faced officer said nothing, but the next morning Andy was sent on his first combat mission. Up until that morning the East Indies had still seemed a game. But before Andy arrived in the combat area he learned several Dutch soldiers had been killed there only recently. The Dutch reinforcements that included Andy were not in a merciful mood. In spite of all his commando training, he soon came to appreciate that firepower was everything. When the Dutch encountered enemy guerillas they showered metal from their weapons into their adversaries. Each soldier exhausted clip after clip of bullets. If their enemy hunkered down in a ditch or behind a fallen tree, they rained mortar shells or hand grenades on them. Andy could scarcely believe he now regularly walked around dead bodies. Only the flies beat him to the bloody victims. Moments before the onslaught, the enemy guerillas had been alive, perhaps cautiously on the move or perhaps chattering happily away.

"Then moments later they are dead," said Andy in awe.

Andy began to drink alcohol now with other soldiers

when they were not on patrol or locked in combat. The alcohol had a nice, numbing effect. Then when he went back into combat and began to lose buddies he got meaner and meaner. In the villages he drank more and more. Sometimes in camp when he could neither fight nor drink he ran off across the paddies or into the jungle. Always he got that wonderful feeling of elation that only running gave him. He ran until he dropped.

Still, he retained a shrewdness. He wasn't going to let his effort in recording the names and addresses of seventy-two families back in Holland go to waste. He wrote them diligently. Most sent him tributes. He was one commando who regularly got packages of treats in the mail. His buddies were cut from the same cloth, full of high energy and bold, but they were amazed by his industry. He fought, he drank, he ran, he wrote letters. He parceled out goodies to his buddies. "Do you ever sleep?" asked a fellow commando.

In July 1947 the Dutch launched an all-out campaign against the PNI. They were determined to root them out of every village. The PNI had two choices, to fight to the death or to go back to rice farming. In just two weeks the PNI was almost shattered. The Dutch were within days of squelching them completely. Then the United Nations negotiated a cease-fire. Soldiers like Andy became very bitter because they knew the PNI would rebuild during the cease-fire. Soldiers like Andy knew also that the PNI—and the Communists—would violate the cease-fire with skirmish after skirmish.

But nothing made the Dutch commandos angrier than land mines. Mines were left by cowards. "Commandos fight face to face, hand to hand," grumbled Andy. One day

Andy's unit drove through a small peaceful-looking village. Suddenly his friend Arnie was obliterated by a landmine in the village street! His body was scattered all over. The mine had been set by the PNI, or perhaps the Communists. Who could be sure? But at that point it didn't matter. The commandos decided then and there the villagers had to know about the mine. Otherwise how could they have avoided it themselves? Andy and his unit became angrier and angrier. If the villagers had warned them, Arnie would be alive. The silence of the villagers could not go unpunished. The commandos went berserk and annihilated the village. Bullets ripped through every hut. Andy's blood thirst stopped only when he came upon a woman and her baby lying in pool of blood. The baby had been feeding at her breast. "One bullet killed them both," observed Andy.

He drank more and more, the better to blunt his nasty memories. He became more bitter as he realized how the United Nations had robbed the Dutch of any possible victory. The Dutch had dropped into third place. The real struggle now seemed to be between the PNI and the Communists. Meanwhile the Dutch army continued to throw its young men into the meat grinder. More and more of Andy's buddies were killed. He and his buddies became wilder and wilder in their battles. Weren't they all going to be killed anyway? They adopted an insane slogan: "Get smart—lose your mind!"

Andy began wearing a bright yellow hat into combat. He was saying: "Here I am. Kill me if you can!" Once he ran far ahead of his outfit and burst upon ten enemy soldiers. "Give up; you're surrounded!" he screamed at them in a dialect of Javanese. Cowed, they dropped their weapons. But how long could he survive such suicidal antics? It seemed he kept his sanity now only because of a pet. In the market at Jakarta he bought a wou-wou. The wou-wou stood almost three feet tall and walked on its bowlegs while holding its arms out like a tightrope walker. It was all white fluffy fur except for its small black face. Some called it a monkey, but the wou-wou was actually a gibbon, a kind of ape. Being an ape it was much smarter than a monkey. It bonded to Andy. It had virtually sold itself to him by mugging and grinning at him at the market. Back at camp the wou-wou kept almost everyone in Andy's barracks in stitches. But Andy made a horrible discovery several weeks later. His wou-wou winced in pain if anyone or anything touched its waist. Brushing back the white fur, Andy discerned a ridge around its waist. Apparently something had been put there some time ago and it was now actually embedded under the skin. With a razor blade Andy cut the skin and removed the object. "A wire, little friend. Now the pain will stop."

When the wou-wou recovered it was bonded even closer to Andy. Often Andy would dash off into the forest to run. The wou-wou followed as long as its lungs held out, but finally it would hurl itself onto his back. Then it rode on his shoulders until Andy's lungs gave out. As Andy sprawled on the forest floor the wou-wou caroused in the trees. When Andy jogged back to camp his pet was on his shoulders again. Andy's life became a succession of bloody skirmishes, barroom drunks, and camp recuperations with his pet.

The routine was broken by a letter from his brother Ben. "He's writing on and on about a funeral," muttered Andy without feeling. Then it hit him. Mama had died! Somehow the first notice of her death had been lost in the mail. Ben's letter assumed he already knew. Andy brooded. Why hadn't he been nicer to Mama? He had felt nothing when he had said goodbye to her in Holland. How could he have been so foolish? Now he had one more unpleasant memory to blunt with alcohol.

He had been in the East Indies for over two years. One night while drunk he wrote a bitter letter to Thile. He wrote that he never prayed. He had no use for God. He wrote her that he told dirty jokes, the filthier the better. He drank until he fell down dead drunk. He killed natives—not just soldiers, but women and children. Oh, the terrible things he had done! The next morning Andy stuffed the letter deep into his duffel bag. In spite of his crushing headache, he realized he couldn't send such a letter to Thile.

The weapons the Dutch used got better and better. Now every soldier in the Dutch East Indies carried a Belgian semiautomatic rifle. They carried many clips for their new weapons and each clip held ten .30-caliber missiles of death. A regular rifle company could spray thousands of bullets per minute at the enemy! Yet the war worsened for the Dutch. They would have been vastly superior in a conventional battle. But the PNI and the Communist guerillas would not fight that way. In February 1949 Andy had a feeling the end was near. PNI were fighting the Dutch near the capital city of Jakarta. He was so sure something terrible was going to happen he had a friend drive him and his wou-wou deep into a forest. Andy stepped out of the Jeep onto the forest trail. His inseparable wou-wou was beside him. Andy crouched and looked into its eyes. This was goodbye. The wou-wou must have understood because as Andy sped away, it just stood in the Jeep's trail and watched. It made no effort to follow.

four

O n the outskirts of Jakarta Andy's unit ran into an
ambush.

The PNI was much bolder. They smelled victory, and few of the Dutch soldiers doubted the outcome either. Andy's unit was ambushed in a bad place. They were marching along ridges between rice paddies. Realizing enemy soldiers were on three sides, the Dutch commandos dashed for cover. Suddenly Andy, the inexhaustible runner, went down. Blood trickled out of his right boot. "I'm hit," he said numbly.

A buddy dragged him down into a paddy. They were safe there in the muck. The enemy would not rush them as the Dutch commandos had too much firepower. But Andy eventually had to be taken out, and he heard bullets whistle around him as two medics lugged him out on a stretcher. He made a nice target with his bright yellow hat. He wondered why he didn't get a bullet through the head.

When the doctors peeled off his boot later in a field hospital, he realized a bullet through the head would have been too easy. His ankle was such a mess the medics debated whether or not to amputate. So this was his punishment for killing! Whether they amputated or not, he, the man who felt good only when he ran, would be a cripple!

Andy recuperated in a hospital run by Franciscan nuns. He had a huge cast on his ankle. When his buddies came to visit they brought the Bible Mama had given him, the Bible he had not looked at in over two years. But he had little time to reflect on his spiritual condition. In his duffel bag his buddies had found the bitter, self-incriminating letter Andy had written to Thile—and they had mailed it! Well, he could forget any parcels from that family!

Andy's experiences had changed him little. To him, life was a series of random happenings. The alert, the prepared, scrambled to survive. Just how he would manage as a cripple he wasn't sure, but he knew how to spend his time in the hospital most profitably. He wrote letters to his dozens of families in Holland—but not to Thile's family, of course.

Andy was wrong about Thile. She wrote him a tender response to his bitter letter. Apparently she saw him as a lost sheep. "Christ will take you just as you are," she promised. This religious stuff meant nothing to Andy, but he was delighted Thile had forgiven him. He had thought about her a lot. She was beautiful and sweet. She would make a very good wife, in spite of her religious beliefs. He glanced at the Bible his buddies brought him. He had left it on a table. Of course he never opened it. It was there to impress the nuns. Some of them were very attractive, especially Sister Patrice.

The cheerfulness of the nuns impressed him, too. How

could they be so cheerful while doing such thankless work? Who would sing and hum while emptying bedpans? Why weren't they cynical and depressed like he was? He put the question to his favorite, Sister Patrice.

"How can you be so cheerful?" he asked.

"It's the love of Christ," she said with some surprise. "But you know that, Andrew. It's all right there in your Bible."

"Of course. . ." he mumbled.

Perhaps reading the Bible was a way for Andy to get better acquainted with Sister Patrice. And it would impress Thile, too. Besides that, he was bored. His buddies had stopped coming to visit, and for good reason. Their time was limited, and Andy reminded them too much of what might happen to them. Sadly, many of them stopped coming because they had been killed. So Andy began reading the Bible. Yawning, he leafed through the thin pages until he found page one.

"In the beginning God created the heaven and the earth," he read.

One of the sisters who noticed him reading his Bible mentioned that Ignatius of Loyola was a Spanish soldier wounded in a battle with the French in the year 1521. During his recuperation he turned to religious books out of boredom. He found that Christianity seemed to answer all his questions. He was a compulsive man. If Christianity had all the answers, should not a man pursue its truths to the very limit of his understanding? Eventually he became the founder of the Jesuit order.

"But I thought you sisters were Franciscans," answered Andy densely.

The sister smiled patiently. She then quoted the prayer by the founder of her order, Francis of Assisi:

Lord, make me an instrument of Thy peace.
Where there is hate, may I bring love;
Where offense, may I bring pardon;
May I bring union in place of discord;
Truth, replacing error;
Faith, where once there was doubt;
Hope, for despair;
Light, where was darkness;
Joy to replace sadness.
Make me not to so crave to be loved as to love.
Help me to learn that in giving I may receive;
In forgetting self, I may find life eternal.

"Is that what you Franciscans believe or do all Catholics believe that?" asked Andy. "What was that last item: 'in forgetting self, I may find life eternal'?"

"Yes," said the sister, smiling.

Andy was surprised by the Bible. The Bible told great stories. He didn't remember it being so entertaining when he first heard the stories as a rambunctious boy back in Sint Pancras. There were many mysteries embedded in it, too. Andy was as overconfident about the Bible as anything else. He figured he could solve any mystery in the Bible. The trees of knowledge and of life? Easy. The sudden appearance of Melchizedek? No problem. Andy glibly spun out an answer for every mystery—but only in his own mind. With Sister Patrice and Thile he would humbly ask their interpretation. He had to admit their answers usually differed from the ones he had dreamed up. The easiest part to understand was the New Testament. Although miraculous, it seemed very straightforward. Andy began to wonder: Could this miraculous story of Jesus be true? Did God really become human to save mankind? It was just too wild a story, even for a wild man like Andy. Besides, the Bible had brought him no joy like he saw in Sister Patrice. He certainly felt no joy the day the cast came off his ankle. His magnificent ankle was a wretched mess! "Just try to walk on an ankle that is as flexible as concrete," he muttered bitterly after trying to walk the first time.

One day Sister Patrice was unusually serious. "You'll soon be leaving us, Andy. I'd like to tell you a story."

"Certainly," answered Andy, appreciating how pretty she was without makeup.

"Do you know how the Javans capture monkeys?"

"No. . ." Andy said, lying. Who knew more about monkeys and apes than he? But what could be nicer than watching a cheerful, lively face that was also very pretty?

"The natives take a very large, heavy coconut and bore a small hole in it. After they drain the milk they put a pebble inside the coconut. Then they wait in the bushes for a monkey to come down out of the trees to investigate the coconut. Eventually a monkey will come down. The hole is just large enough for the monkey's hand. He reaches inside and feels the pebble. But he can't take his hand out when he clutches the pebble. The hole isn't big enough. Do you know what happens when the natives come out of the bushes?"

"No," lied Andy again.

"The monkey will not surrender his pebble. And he is

51

easily caught because he can't lug the heavy coconut into the tree."

"Quite a story, Sister Patrice," said Andy, stifling a yawn.

"Maybe you are like that monkey, Andy."

"What!"

"What are you holding on to? What is it that will cost you your soul?"

Andy tried to remain agreeable but he didn't see what the story had to do with him. Oh yes, he remembered from his Bible reading how the prophet Nathan had opened King David's eyes with a parable that turned out to be about the king himself. But now that Sister Patrice had tried to do that with Andy, he didn't much appreciate it. What was she talking about? What was he clutching like a monkey? And what was all this talk about a soul?

He was glad to be dismissed from the hospital. The night before Andy sailed back to Holland he got together with commandos who had first come to the East Indies with him back in 1946. Of the original company only eight were still alive! For each one still alive, ten of their buddies had died. Yet Andy fell right back into his old habits. In spite of his bad ankle he made the rounds of the sleazy bars on a cane until he got falling-down drunk with the others. "Maybe I have hold of something or something has hold of me, but who cares, Sister Patrice?" he crowed in a drunken stupor to his puzzled buddies.

Almost on his twenty-first birthday, May 11, 1949, Andy sailed for Holland. Days later Papa, Ben, Cornelius, Maartje, and Geltje welcomed him home. Geltje was married and Ben was about to be wed. Andy struggled on his lame leg to Mama's grave. There he broke down and told

Mama how hopeless his life was now. He pleaded for answers. What was he going to do? But he pulled himself together after he left her graveside. Visits to old neighbors were small comfort. He discovered the combination of his uniform and his cane reminded people they had lost their precious empire. The Dutch had truly loved the East Indies. They seemed relieved when he left. Only the Whetstras put him at ease. But when Mr. Whetstra started talking about praying Andy blew up. Embarrassed by his outburst, he left. Then he visited his old friend Kees. Kees was studying for the ministry. Andy was appalled. Couldn't Kees think of anything better to do than that? fumed Andy to himself after he left him.

All Andy's Bible reading had not affected his heart at all. He felt more and more like a fish out of water. He was not yet out of the army, and he was glad when the army sent him to Doorn for rehabilitation. There he had physical therapy. He also puttered around vocational courses, none of which interested him. For some strange reason he was forced to sit in a class and try to make pottery on a wheel. It was called occupational therapy. Andy rarely shaped his lumps of clay into anything recognizable, certainly not into actual pots. All his failures he called ashtrays. Andy hated the class and showed his fellow potters just how nasty he could get. One poor fellow got Andy's lump of clay on the side of his head!

On his first weekend leave he did not return to Sint Pancras but took a bus to Gorkum. There he was reunited with Thile. He admitted his religious life had come to standstill. "But God is not at a standstill," objected Thile.

Andy brushed off the remark. Then for the second time

since he returned to Holland he whined to someone about his misfortunes. Nothing was going right for him. What was he going to do? The tough guy, the bully, had crumbled. But instead of winning Thile's sympathy he angered her.

"Maybe you're smoking too much," she said sourly.

He left her on an angry note. It seemed he could get along with no one. In September 1949 the soldiers at the hospital were invited to a revival. The girl who invited them was very pretty, so Andy went with Pier, another soldier in rehabilitation. They had many drinks first. Once at the revival Pier and Andy, both drunk, sat at the back, snickering and laughing all through the meeting.

"Brothers and sisters!" boomed a man at the podium. "We have two men here tonight who are chained by powers of the dark world."

The man, whom Andy quickly dubbed "rat-face" because he had a thin face with deep-set eyes, began to pray for the two drunken soldiers. The more he prayed for the dark powers to release the men, the louder Andy and Pier guffawed. Finally in exasperation the speaker called for a hymn. Andy was stunned by the volume of the singers. It seemed everyone in the tent wanted to drown out the two drunken pests. Over and over a refrain boomed from the voices: "Let my people go!" Andy suddenly sobered. It seemed he was hearing "let him go!" Yes, let me go, he was suddenly screaming inside himself. He wasn't at all happy with himself when the revival ended. Surely he wasn't feeling guilty, was he? After all the things he had done? He had killed people.

Later he began to wonder if the hymn were like a prayer for him. Could all those people have been praying for the dark powers to let him go? He was surprised with himself. He wasn't used to such insights. Yet the next day in occupational therapy he actually made some very nice pottery. Perhaps some dark thing had let him go. He couldn't remember anything quite as miraculous in his own life since he had started running many years ago. Later he picked up his Bible and discovered that many of its mysteries were clear to him now. He did not have to dream up some bluster to explain them. What had happened? Not only did he understand the Bible, but he now had an insatiable appetite for its very words. While the craving itself gave him joy, his greatest pleasure was reading the Bible. The people in the Old Testament were so wonderful, yet so flawed. Then, at last, in the New Testament came the perfect man Isaiah had promised in the Old Testament!

" 'Wonderful Counselor, Mighty God, Everlasting Father, Prince of Peace,' " quoted Andy. "Yes, Jesus."

By November 1949 he was classified as rehabilitated and released from the army. He still did not know what he was going to do. But he did know he had a new thirst: a knowledge of God. Back at Sint Pancras, Andy, who had always disdained church services, became an enthusiastic regular on Sunday mornings. Then he found he had to go Sunday evenings. Then he added Wednesday evenings, too. He felt he was very close to something, something that would at last set him free. He bought a bicycle, telling everyone it was to strengthen his lame leg. But he strengthened his leg by pedaling to Alkmaar on Monday nights for the Salvation Army service. Then on Tuesday night he barreled all the way into Amsterdam for a Baptist service. Occasionally he saw Thile. She was worried about his new piety. She knew he was compulsive about his interests. Would he become a self-righteous, Bible-quoting bore?

His family was worried, too. Papa confided to Andy's siblings in a window-rattling whisper, "Andy might be suffering 'shell shock'!"

But Andy knew he was so close to something very vital. One blizzard-howling night in January 1950 he snuggled under his blankets in the loft. He knew outside the snow was sweeping across the polders. The icy atmosphere in the loft seemed crystalline and pure. Suddenly he knew the answer to all his problems, all his anguish. At last he understood. The monkey let go of the pebble, and Andy surrendered to God.

"Lord, if You will show the way, I will follow You. Amen."

For the first time in years Andy awoke with joy in his heart. He had never felt this magnitude of joy! And yet he couldn't tell his family. They regarded his interest in religion almost as an illness from the war. But there were some he could talk to in Sint Pancras. He could certainly tell the Whetstras. He was disappointed when they accepted it so casually. They hinted it was a well-traveled road Andy had just taken. They used the phrase "born again." But they were happy for him. The other person in Sint Pancras Andy could talk to was his old friend Kees. After all, Kees was studying for the ministry.

"Hmmm, a classic case of crisis conversion," mulled Kees upon hearing the good news.

"What?"

"It will be most interesting to observe your future actions, Andrew. . ."

"Well, what can I expect from this?"

"Perhaps a response-in-depth."

Kees seemed to be in an ivory tower. Andy could understand almost none of his religious jargon. Nevertheless, he had someone he could talk to in Sint Pancras. After a while Kees dropped his professorial demeanor to explain that a crisis conversion occurred when the person was in the depths of despair. A response-in-depth meant a spiritual awakening in the person as profound as the despair. Armed with this new knowledge and this new joy in his heart, Andy bicycled to see Thile when the weather cleared.

She was not pleased. "It sounds peculiar, Andy. Like one of those conversions at a revival meeting."

Andy began to realize that Thile and his own family were suspicious of evangelicals. They had a rigid Dutch Reformed view of what a Christian should be. Their view may well have been the right one; Andy didn't know. But he was thirsty for the Word. He listened with an open mind to the views of Dutch Reformed, Baptist, and other Protestant denominations. He wasn't open to the hierarchy of Catholicism but after being pampered, even counseled, by the Franciscan Sisters, he respected their dedication.

It was that openness that led Andy and Kees to take the bus a few weeks later into Amsterdam to hear the well-known evangelist Arne Donker. Before Donker preached, a woman working in the slums of Paris spoke. She told a parablelike story of a streetworker who neglected to fill in a few paving stones. Because of a missing stone, a man was thrown from his horse and killed. Because of the man's death his wife and daughters were left destitute. They turned to prostitution and lured many a good man away from his own wife.

"Oh, how many lives were ruined because this street-worker did not finish his job!" the small woman cried out. "Do you have some unfinished work?"

Andy and Kees looked at each other approvingly. Yes, it was a good story told with passion. They listened approvingly to Arne Donker's sermon, too. Near the end of the meeting Donker announced that he felt God was telling him someone in the audience wanted to become a missionary. Like most successful evangelists, Donker made all the listeners in the audience feel he was talking to them personally. Certainly Andy and Kees felt that way, but they didn't want to be missionaries. They panicked and tried to leave. Neither could remember who nudged whom first. Nor could they remember who got up to leave first.

"There they are!" boomed Arne Donker. "Praise God! There are two of them!"

Andy wanted to scream at the top of his lungs, "There's been a huge mistake here!" But instead, numb with disbelief, Andy found himself trudging—he still had a bad limp—down the aisle of the meeting hall with Kees. What had happened? Was this God's hand, or simply Arne Donker's skill? It was certainly Donker whom Andy heard saying a prayer over him and Kees, thanking God that these two young men had committed themselves to mission work.

After the meeting adjourned a beaming Donker took them aside. After he learned their names he gushed, "Now, Kees and Andrew, my young missionaries, I will give you your first assignment!"

"First assignment?" responded Kees numbly.

"Where are you from?"

"Sint Pancras. . ."

"Excellent. You must hold an open-air meeting there."

"When?" yelped Andy.

"This coming Saturday. In the afternoon in front of the mayor's house." Donker had a knowing look on his face. "Oh, come now. I'll be there with you. Don't you remember the Lord saying in the Book of Matthew, 'Neither do people light a lamp and put it under a bowl.' It's time for you young men to show your light!"

"But in our hometown?" whined Kees. "Jesus also said in the Book of Matthew, 'Only in his hometown and in his own house is a prophet without honor.'"

"Oh, you know your Scripture, too!" exclaimed Donker. "Wonderful! Here is what I want you two to speak on. Kees, your topic is 'He sought me.' Andrew, your topic is 'He found me.' Then I will conclude on the theme 'He set me free.' Oh, I can hardly wait for Saturday!"

On the bus ride back Andy was paralyzed. Street preachers were regarded by rigid Dutch Reformed believers as crackpots! And all the people he cared about were Dutch Reformed believers. What would Papa think? What would his sisters and brothers think? And Thile! Oh, she would be embarrassed to tears when she heard about it. Andy had never been so frightened. Not even dodging bullets in the East Indies had frightened him so much. Well, he would know Saturday whether he had been reborn. Was he a new man or not?

Back at Sint Pancras, still numb, he wrote out his tiny

sermon on "He found me." He memorized every word. All week long he practiced in front of a mirror. At times he became giddy from fright. He cracked jokes to the wildly appreciative audience in his imagination. Then he would sober. He would never be able to deliver this sermon. Then he fantasized no one would come. Neither he nor Kees had mentioned it to anyone. Yes, surely no one would come. Surely he could deliver his tiny sermon to the nonjudgmental dikes and polders! "Take this cup from me," he prayed at moments of extreme despair. Then at times he realized how cowardly he was acting. For over two years he had fought like a madman in the East Indies, never giving anyone a chance to label him a coward. But now he was every ounce a coward, and all his agonizing could not stop the clock.

Saturday afternoon brought a scenario that he had never dared to imagine. It seemed everyone in Sint Pancras was gathered to hear these street preachers! Andy was suffering from stage fright of the worst kind. His ears were ringing. He felt like his face was on fire. Then the moment came for Kees to get up and deliver his sermon. Andy could not distinguish a single word. When his own dread moment arrived, he limped forward. Solemnly he began to regurgitate the words he had memorized. He heard his own voice. He sounded like a dead man.

Abruptly he abandoned his rehearsed sermon. "I did some terrible things over in the East Indies," he confessed. "I was lost when I came back. I felt dirty. Guilt over the past and anxiety about the future hung on me like chains." Suddenly he felt his fear drain away. The truth had set him free. "One January night I laid my burden at the feet of

Jesus. I surrendered myself to Him. . ."

Andy continued by saying how he felt Arne Donker had tricked him into volunteering to be a missionary. "But you know I might just surprise everyone. . . ."

five

Andy's inquiries into missionary work resulted only in discouragement.

Becoming a missionary for the Dutch Reformed church seemed a mountain to climb. First he would have to be ordained as a minister. Officials of the church informed him it would take twelve years to make up the schooling he had lost during the war as well as to study the necessary theology. Thile was the one who had narrowed his inquiry to the Dutch Reformed church. She advised Andy to get a job in the meantime and do whatever good works he could at home. Andy suspected she was pleased with the result. She didn't want him to be a missionary.

"But where can I find work?" he asked his own family.

"My husband Arie will put in a good word for you at the chocolate factory," volunteered his sister Geltje.

"Yes, why not?" answered Andy.

Andy still had pain when he walked, but for short

periods now he could walk without a limp. What was he waiting for? He had been home now for almost one year. He would soon turn twenty-two. He had to get the war behind him.

His interview at the chocolate factory in nearby Alkmaar went well. He was hired to cart boxes of chocolates from the cavernous assembly room to the shipping platform. From a timekeeper in the assembly room he had to pick up a work order. The work order listed a certain number of boxes for the various assortments of candy that he had to load on his cart. The assembly room was full of women at conveyor belts. He felt relieved when he saw all the women wearing aprons and head scarves. This would surely be a very pleasant job.

"Well, girls, look at the new meat!" yelled one woman.

What followed made Andy think he was in a nightmare. He had never heard such filthy talk outside the army. And women were talking that way! One woman, Greetje, was the worst. She leered at Andy. She peppered him with filth, with references to sodomy, bestiality, and other perversions. He seemed in a daze as he wheeled the boxes out of the assembly room to the shipping room. The shipping room was full of men. They watched Andy warily. They seemed to know—probably from Arie—that a war-shattered commando trained to kill was no one to tease. After Andy delivered the boxes to the shipping room, he took a receipt for the boxes to the timekeeper. The timekeeper gave him another work order to fill in the assembly room. This time Andy noticed the timekeeper was a trim blond woman so young she appeared to be in her teens. She smiled warmly at Andy.

"The women tease every newcomer that way," she said. "They'll stop after a day or two."

"Thanks," gushed Andy. "That's good to hear."

The blond timekeeper jolted him. Her eyes seemed to change with the light. Were they green, hazel, or brown? He stopped staring and left to fill the work order. All day long he shoved the cart back and forth between the assembly room where the women teased him with raunchy taunts to the loading area where the men watched him with suspicion. Near the end of the day he could no longer hide his limp.

"Whose bed did you just fall out of?" yelled Greetje.

"Outside Jakarta," he mumbled without thinking.

"Oh, the East Indies," she said, her face lighting up. "Girls, we have a war hero in our midst!"

"Oh, no," groaned Andy.

Now Greetje was merciless. She peppered Andy with every anecdote about every perversion she thought was practiced in the East Indies or the entire Orient for that matter. That Andy had indeed indulged in some of these disgusting activities didn't make him feel any better. Now the women had something else to tease him about. He would have to learn to grin and bear it. More important, he would have to hold his tongue. They continued to tease him longer than the timekeeper said they would. The only bright spots in the entire workday were the times he had to get a new work order from the pretty blond timekeeper. She alone made the whole work experience worthwhile. He learned her name was Corrie van Dam. He began to worry about such a nice young woman being in such a workplace.

After one month he said nervously to Corrie, "You are too young to be hearing such filthy remarks."

"They're not such a bad lot really," she replied. "Because of the wars Holland has a great shortage of men, you know. These poor women are lonely. And the poor souls think that kind of rude behavior is the way to attract men."

What insight! What compassion! So young and yet so wise. Andy became even more infatuated with Corrie van Dam. When he went to one of the youth meetings that the British evangelist Sidney Wilson was holding in Holland on Saturdays, he was thrilled to see Corrie there, too. Soon there was a regular group of young people from the chocolate factory that attended the meetings.

One of the youths was Amy, a blind girl who worked on the assembly line. She was a very bright, determined girl. At home Amy punched out letters to other blind people with a Braille-writer. Andy was very fond of her. One day at the factory when he came into the assembly room he noticed Amy crying. Greetje wasn't even looking at her as she sorted chocolates but kept up her banter.

For Andy's benefit Greetje added nastily, "Yes, Amy, you know a blind girl can never be absolutely sure just who it was she had relations with. . . ."

Andy felt a rage he had not felt for several years. "Oh, shut up, Greetje! Shut up for keeps!"

Greetje's jaw dropped. She put her hands on her hips. "What did—?" Stopping in midsentence, Greetje must have detected something deadly serious in Andy's eyes.

Andy barked at Greetje, "If you know what's good for you, you will be at the Alkmaar bus depot Saturday morning. Nine sharp!"

Amazingly, Greetje was there Saturday morning. Corrie had been right. The poor soul was starved for company. But she was not subdued just yet. All during the day she kept up her irreverent remarks. "Kids," she snorted. "Kids with dumb conversion stories. Ho hum." When she got too winded from her cynical cracks she read a romance magazine. *How revealing*, thought Andy. *Yes, the poor soul wants romance in her life*. Everything Greetje did showed Andy that Corrie had been completely right in not rejecting supposedly lost souls like her.

When they returned to the Alkmaar bus depot where Andy had left his bike he offered Greetje a ride home. Usually he went with several others to Corrie's home. There Mrs. Van Dam treated them to coffee and cookies, and Mr. van Dam quietly smoked his pipe and enjoyed watching his young guests sing and talk. But today Andy decided to go home so he could offer Greetje a ride. Greetje was suspicious of Andy's offer. Surely Andy was going to rant about Christianity the entire way. But on the other hand it gave her a wonderful opportunity to pepper him with raunch. And what fun she could have with the story of this bicycle ride back in the assembly room!

"All right, Andy," she said, looking at Corrie suggestively. "I've been wanting to find out for a long time just what you look like without your clothes."

Off they went, with Andy praying silently for wisdom. Suddenly he sensed this was no time to talk about Christianity. He would show Greetje decent Christian warmth and hospitality. He talked about every sight they saw on the way, trying to draw her out. They had many experiences in common. Surviving World War II was one of them. Yes, Greetje remembered very well eating tulip bulbs instead of potatoes. Yes, her schooling had ended, too. Yes, she, too, had a brother who was an Onderduiker, who just ran off one day and never came back until the war was over. When Andy let her off she actually smiled at him. Under that raunchy exterior was a woman crying out for affection.

The next Monday morning Greetje was strangely silent. "Bad time of the month!" she snapped at a puzzled questioner.

But at lunch in the cafeteria she sat down by Andy, looking very uncomfortable. Oh, how hard it must have been for her to do this, Andy knew. She glanced around to be sure no one else was near enough to hear. She still wore her cynical, sarcastic face, but it didn't match her words.

"You know at first I was glad you didn't preach to me Saturday when you gave me a ride home. But the more I thought about it, the more depressed I became. I thought maybe you didn't preach to me because you decided I was beyond redemption. And I began wondering if I were beyond forgiveness. All day Saturday those kids talked about repenting and being forgiven and starting over. Is it too late for me? I wondered. Am I too far lost? Finally last night I prayed to God to let me start over again. I hate what I am. I cried all night. But today I feel different, like maybe I can start over again."

Greetje had changed. She kept up her bluster in the assembly room, but the filth was gone. She was a natural leader. Now she directed her energy into doing good. It was Greetje who organized a prayer group. It was Greetje who collected money for fellow workers with problems. Andy had seen this miraculous conversion of a desperate soul, and he had maybe even caused it. He was more determined than ever to be a missionary. But the world intervened.

The owner of the chocolate factory called him into his office. "Sit down, Andrew," he said. "I want to discuss your future."

"Thank you, sir," answered Andy nervously.

"Tests you took when we hired you indicate you are of high intelligence."

"Really, sir?" answered Andy. Years ago, the old, over-confident Andy wouldn't even have considered that a compliment but the simple, undeniable truth. Now he was humbled. After all he had been wrong about life for twenty-two years.

"Yes, but intelligence isn't enough for what I'm looking for. I need leadership, too. They tell me you are a leader."

"They do, sir?"

"I want you look around the factory. Tell me which type of work you like the most, and we will train you for it. All I ask in exchange for the training and promotion is that you commit to the job for at least two years."

"Thank you, sir." Andy excused himself.

Two years. This was a wonderful opportunity, but it would cost him precious time. When was he going to get on with his missionary work?

Still, the temptation was too great; soon Andy began training in the personnel office. He would be a job analyst. That meant he met every new employee to discuss with them what they were suited for. Somehow, at the same time, he felt bound to delve into their religious prefer-ences. No, he wouldn't shove Christianity down their throats.

But what if they were troubled? Was he not going to counsel them?

Andy promised God that after two years he would get on with his mission work. That meant preparing for it now. He gave up smoking so he could buy books. The van der Bijl home had only two books: the Bible and a hymnbook. The Bible was magnificent—it had changed his life—but he needed more to prepare himself for mission work. He bought grammar books for German and English. He purchased a Bible commentary to compare with his own interpretations of passages. He added a church history and other books he could afford.

Meanwhile he consulted the British evangelist Sidney Wilson. "With my limited education, Reverend Wilson, I fear I may never do mission work."

"Have you not heard of Gladys Aylward?"

"No. . ."

"She was a tiny, mousy parlor maid almost thirty years old. The mission people told her that at her age she could never learn a foreign language. She went to China on her own and became an assistant to a missionary. Today she speaks Mandarin Chinese like a native. Although she disdains fame, she is famous anyway. That tiny woman escorted one hundred orphan children through the mountains during the war to save them. Don't ever say 'I can't'! Have you heard of William Carey?"

"Isn't he called the 'father of modern missionary work' or something like that?"

"Yes, and he was a poor shoemaker with little formal education."

"I see."

"I'm not telling you to go it alone or to found a mission movement. No, I recommend an English organization called in English the 'Worldwide Evangelization Crusade'."

"That's quite a mouthful."

"That's why most people just say 'WEC'. But the long and short of it is that they will train you for two years. After that you will be sent into an area where there are no missionaries."

Andy was burning with desire now. He learned the WEC had been founded by a missionary named C. T. Studd. Studd was one of the so-called Cambridge Seven: In 1885 seven privileged young men at Cambridge University, who were also star cricket players, caused a tremendous sensation by volunteering to go to China to work for Hudson Taylor's China Inland Mission. Studd lost his health there, went to India for a few years, then to Africa. His organization in Africa, 'Heart of Africa,' became the Worldwide Evangelization Crusade. He died in Africa in 1931.

Studd had a famous quote among missionaries:

> "Some wish to live within the sound of church
> and chapel bell. I wish to run a rescue mission
> within a yard of hell!"[1]

While Andy was more and more fascinated with the lives of missionaries, in his spare time he studied English more than any other subject. His enthusiasm drew in his friend Kees. Kees had no two-year obligation at a factory. To Andy's utter amazement it was Kees who was soon enrolled at the training school of WEC in Glasgow, Scotland. And it seemed no time later at all that Kees was in Glasgow writing letters to Andy. Imagine! Kees was at that very moment in Glasgow, where the great missionary David Livingstone had studied medicine before doing his miraculous missionary work in Africa! Now that was adventure!

When Andy finally fulfilled his obligation at the chocolate factory, he still didn't feel ready to become a missionary. He studied his books. He continued to focus on English, even taking English lessons from his former teacher, Miss Meekle. In September 1952 Andy walked far out in the polders. He needed plenty of space to talk to God. He knelt along a canal. After much prayer he realized he had put too many restrictions on beginning his missionary service. He had to be like the parlor maid Gladys Aylward and just forge ahead.

"Blast all the qualifications and prerequisites and rules and regulations!" he cried out loud.

Then a miraculous thing happened. Andy stood up, at the same time boldly telling God that this would be his first step in complete obedience. Afterward he remembered it as his "Step of Yes." As he stepped forward his bad ankle popped like a gunshot. For just a moment his faith left him. Oh no, I've injured my ankle even more! he thought desperately. But it was just the opposite. His ankle had flexibility in it again! That night he walked to and from a youth meeting in Alkmaar, a round trip of ten miles! His ankle was weak, but it was functioning properly again.

The next day he filled out an application for the next training class at WEC. It was a time of new beginnings as his friend Corrie van Dam quit the chocolate factory almost the same day to start nursing school. Weeks later, he was accepted to begin at WEC in May 1953. Andy purchased his passage to London for April, when he would meet the directors of the mission.

But not everything went smoothly. Thile wrote him a cold letter requesting that he not write her again. Apparently the WEC embarrassed her. But that letter was easier to accept than the one he received from the WEC. They had no vacancy for May 1953 after all. Andy should reapply in 1954.

"Oh, no," said Corrie. "What are you going to do now?"

"I'll go anyway!" Just exactly what Gladys Aylward would have done!

As he said his farewells at the chocolate factory, he knew he had not converted everyone. There was one small gray-haired woman who was a card-carrying member of the Communist party. By definition the Communists did not believe in God. They were atheists, and most were defiant atheists. Andy had sparred with the woman many times. Still, he wanted to say goodbye to her, even if he knew what to expect. Her usual banter was filled with Communist references: Her pay was "slave wages;" Queen Juliana was an "oppressor." But her nastiest comments she saved for Christianity.

"You may be leaving, Andrew, but unfortunately your lies are not! You've poisoned too many people here with your Christian fairy tale."

"It's God's story. And God gives them the choice to believe or not to believe."

"These people are not trained in dialectics," she sputtered. "Who wouldn't want to believe in God—" She cut herself short. She was almost crying she was so angry. Or was she sad?

In April 1953 Andy arrived in London. His first discovery was that he could not understand the English people, nor could they understand his English. He showed a taxi driver a piece of paper with the address of the WEC headquarters. Minutes later he presented himself at the headquarters. Fortunately they had a man there who knew some Dutch.

"But we wrote you that there was no vacancy for this year," the man explained.

"Yes, I got the letter," said Andy.

"Ahhh. . . ."

The man didn't seem upset. In fact, he smiled. Apparently he had seen this attitude in missionary candidates before. "It can't be done" was not in their make-up. The headquarters of the WEC not only took Andy in but put him to work. Soon he was painting the outside of the building! All England was abuzz on June 2, 1953, when young Elizabeth was crowned queen. And where was Andy? He was perched high on the side of the WEC headquarters building, paintbrush in hand. More than a painter, Andy participated in morning prayers and evening devotionals, too.

One of the most important things he learned during his stay at the headquarters was the practice of "Quiet Time." This consisted of rising early enough in the morning to have plenty of time to pray and read the Bible. This practice did for Andy what he once thought only running did. His reasoning became lucid. His emotions became tranquil.

After a few weeks at the headquarters Andy went to the shire of Kent near London to live with William Hopkins

74

and his wife. He was told to call them "Uncle Hoppy" and "Mother Hoppy." They were true Christians. Although Hopkins was a building contractor, he and his wife gave nearly all their money away. They lived simply and Uncle Hoppy dressed so shabbily even Andy was bothered by his appearance. Uncle Hoppy ran a storefront mission. He preached there, usually to empty chairs, and he insisted Andy preach there also. When it was his turn, Andy took the topic of his sermon from Luke 18. In that passage, when confronted by a blind man on the road to Jericho, Jesus said, "Receive thy sight: thy faith hath saved thee."

"Receive die side: die fade had saved dee," said Andy to Uncle Hoppy, his one perplexed listener.

The "th" sound is unusually difficult for Dutch people. For fourteen minutes Andy held forth with tongue-twisted English. At moments he even saw the humor in it himself. But he honored the solemnity of the occasion, and so did his listener. Afterward Uncle Hoppy congratulated him on his rapidly improving English! Uncle Hoppy was kindness himself. He was not judgmental. He gave away money left and right. Unconditionally. He offered help— even a bed in his home—to anyone, no matter if they were drunks or prostitutes.

Andy's persistence paid off. He was notified he would not have to wait until 1954 to get into the Glasgow training school. He could come for the fall term. So in September 1953 he went to Euston Station in London and boarded the northbound train to Scotland. At the two-story house at 10 Prince Albert Road in Glasgow, Andy was greeted by Kees. Kees took him to his room and introduced him to his three roommates. There were about fifty students—men and women—at the training school, but the women boarded apart. The men were warned never to socialize with the women outside of school.

Before Andy entered the front door he had passed through a wooden archway with the motto "Have Faith in God." The director of the school, Stewart Dinnen, expanded on that theme. "Our graduates have the least financial support of all missionaries. And because we go into areas untouched by other missions we do not have the companionship or support of other missionaries. Yet a missionary cannot do a good job if he is afraid. So, above all else, here you must learn to trust God. If you don't you will surely fail."

Mornings at the training school were spent in traditional missionary preparation. The students studied theology, world religions, and languages. But in the afternoons they learned trades. It was the great David Livingstone who had snapped at a critic that he was no smug frump with a Bible tucked under his arm. He could lay bricks or do anything else that needed to be done. And that was the attitude of this school. The students learned bricklaying, carpentry, plumbing, first aid, hygiene, and motor repair. Men and women both went to a Ford factory to learn how to take a car apart and put it back together again.

And while Andy became adept at all kinds of repairs, somehow he could not avoid a severe physical setback.

six

Andy's back "went out."

He was in constant pain, and at times the pain was almost unbearable. Some mornings he could not comb his hair or dress himself. A few times he was seized by pain so agonizing he fell down. If no one were around, he just had to wait until someone found him. Then he had to be helped into his bed until he recovered. When a physician said surgery was too dangerous, his fellow students prayed for him, even laying hands on him. Nothing seemed to work.

Is this belated punishment for my mad killing days? Andy wondered. But hadn't he been forgiven for his sins when he gave himself to Christ?

Somehow he struggled through his studies. He found comfort in reading Oswald Chambers's devotional book *My Utmost for His Highest.* One passage was especially meaningful to Andy:

"If you are going to be used by God, He will
take you through a multitude of experiences that
are not meant for you at all, they are meant to
make you useful in His hands, and to enable you
to understand what transpires in other souls so
that you will never be surprised at what you come
across."[1]

Yes, Andy reassured himself, this terrible back pain is
surely preparation for some future trial.

Oswald Chambers himself died at a young age from a
ruptured appendix, and in 1954 he had been dead for
many years. When Andy learned that his wife Biddy,
though quite old, was still very much alive in southern
England, he wrote her a letter expressing what great comfort he experienced from her husband's book. In response,
Biddy Chambers graciously invited him to visit. And that's
exactly what he did during the Christmas holidays. During
the visit Andy learned that Biddy was the one who pains-
takingly put *My Utmost for His Highest* together from her
own notes of what her husband spoke and wrote. He was
impressed at what devotion she had shown to her husband
and to Christ.

Back at school Stewart Dinnen asked Andrew, "And
where did you go during the holidays, Andrew?"

"I stayed with Mrs. Oswald Chambers."

"What? You can't do that!"[2]

Andy shrugged. "But I did."

Andy then had another unique experience. His WEC
school sent out teams of five to evangelize throughout
Scotland. Each student was given only a few dollars,

money that was expected to be paid back upon return! Students were not allowed to solicit money, food, or shelter during the trip. That understood, Andy and his four fellow students went off to test their faith in God. They preached all over the rugged Scottish countryside. Amazingly, money always seemed to appear, by letter or from a church group. Often they were given food. Andy would never have believed it possible to survive such a trip without a reserve of money. But they did.

"We went all the way across Scotland to Edinburgh and back," he reflected in astonishment after his return.

After one year Kees was gone. He had graduated and was assigned to a mission in Korea. Andy continued to enjoy his final two years at the school in spite of his severe back problem. His war experience in the East Indies had given him a rare perspective. After all, he was the one Dutch soldier out of ten who had survived the war. Fortified with that knowledge, and the armor of Christ, he could enjoy the school in spite of his affliction. But he saw a potential problem. He was going to put Stewart Dinnen in an uncomfortable position. Andy was going to graduate, but Stewart would probably have to refuse to place him as a WEC missionary because of his chronic disability. That would be a bad precedent for the organization. Andy did not want people whispering that the school would betray a student. There was only one honorable thing to do.

"God, give me guidance," he prayed. "I must leave here, but please give me an alternate plan."

The spring before he was due to graduate he went down into the basement to get his suitcase. Sticking out among the dusty boxes and suitcases like a rose among weeds was a shiny new magazine. It was a Communist magazine, filled with blatant propaganda aimed at westerners. The slick, colorful pages touted a massive youth conference in Warsaw, Poland. Thousands upon thousands of Communist youths would attend, the magazine claimed. Andy remembered the Communist woman at the chocolate factory. In his heart he knew that woman wanted desperately to believe in God. What about all these young people? Weren't many of them like that woman?

That very night he wrote a frank letter to the conference organizers:

> I am training to be a Christian missionary, and would like to come to the youth festival to exchange ideas. I would like to talk about Jesus Christ, and listen to others talk about socialism. Is it possible for me to come under those circumstances?[3]

He mailed it, doubting he would even receive an answer. But he soon had their approval. They were so confident they could convert him to Communism, they were eager to have him there. They enclosed a permit for him. All he had to do was board a special train in Amsterdam on July 15, 1955, that would take him straight to Warsaw, Poland. But it wasn't free, as Andy confided to Uncle Hoppy.

Uncle Hoppy was shocked. "But Poland is behind the Iron Curtain!"

The great British Prime Minister Winston Churchill had popularized that term. After World War II, Russia had oppressed all of eastern Europe, setting up puppet Communist governments. In a memorable speech given in 1946, Churchill said in his inimitable growl, "From Stettin in the Baltic to Trieste in the Adriatic an iron curtain has descended across the continent." Travel in these Communist countries was exceedingly difficult, not to mention dangerous. All hard-line Communist officials were perceived to be as paranoid and murderous as their leader, the Russian dictator Joseph Stalin.

Still, always kind and always enthusiastic, Uncle Hoppy gave Andy the money he needed. He had too much faith in God to discourage Andy. Then Andy went to Stewart Dinnen to say he was withdrawing from the school. It didn't seem so bad now that he had some future plans. Dinnen looked like a man just pardoned from the gallows. With his honorable withdrawal complete, Andy left for Holland and Sint Pancras.

Geltje now had a small boy toddling about the house. Ben lived with his wife in Ermelo, which was on the other side of the Zuider Zee. The Whetstras were in the process of moving to Amsterdam, where their flower export business would be considerably easier. Although Kees was in Korea, Andy visited all the friends he could. He had to mend some fences in Holland, too.

While at school Andy had often been nagged by guilt. Yes, he was forgiven, but he still had to make what reparations he could. He began by writing his brother Ben. In his letter he confessed to robbing his piggy bank. Ben wrote back saying the only debt they had was to love each other. Andy went to the man he had stolen apples from during the war. The man shook his head in disbelief and refused any kind of payment. He understood better than Andy that people were starving in those terrible days. Andy went to a shop where as a twelve year old he had stolen a pocketknife. That man also shook his head in disbelief, but he accepted Andy's payment. Andy made other apologies, too. The German soldiers he had victimized were long gone from Holland. Whether he could have ever admitted to his oppressors he had stolen their weapons and sabotaged their automobile he did not know. Still, trying to right a few of his old wrongs felt cleansing to Andy.

But he was uneasy, too. He was now twenty-seven years old. He was a physical wreck, unmarried, virtually penniless, and with the vaguest future. Just how much do I trust God? he asked himself in weak moments. He did have one thing in his future: the youth conference in Poland.

Aboard the train that left Amsterdam were hundreds of young men and women. Obviously, the magnitude of the youth conference was more than just Communist bluster. It was going to be huge. Andy had packed only a few clothes, but he lugged a heavy suitcase. It was jammed with copies of the thirty-one-page booklet "The Way of Salvation," written in Polish. In spite of the throng on the train Andy felt isolated. These young people were either Communists or flirting with Communism. He prayed, wondering if anyone else around him were doing the same.

Once in Warsaw, Andy was put up in a school classroom full of cots. The routine of the visiting youths was tightly controlled. In the morning they went sightseeing. They saw new schools, high-rise apartments, busy factories, and shops full of goods. In the afternoon they listened to speeches. Andy fumed. He was not going to take three weeks of that force-fed propaganda. It shouldn't be that difficult to slip away to see the real Poland, he reasoned. After all, there are 30,000 of us at the conference!

One morning he rose very early and scurried out of the school into an unvisited neighborhood. Never had he seen such devastation, not in Holland during World War II nor in the East Indies during the war there. Block after block of this "off-limits" Warsaw were piled with brick and plaster rubble. About the only sign of civilization was a path through the rubble. People wandered along the path like lost souls. They wore rags filthier than the hopeless drunks wore in Holland. Yet this scene was taking place ten years after the conclusion of World War II! Communism was a dismal, godless failure. "This is the true Communism," Andy sighed.

Then Andy could scarcely believe his eyes. A small barefoot girl came skipping out of one of the holes in the rubble. People actually lived burrowed inside the mounds of debris! Andy offered the girl one of his booklets. She approached him warily, then snatched the booklet and darted back into the hole. Again Andy's suspicions were confirmed of the failure of the Communist way of life. But how he wished these were not true, because the victims of Communism were living, breathing human beings like the small barefoot girl!

Back at the school that evening he related his excursion to a Dutch Communist named Hans. He told Hans exactly where to go to see the ugliness of Warsaw. Hans glared at him angrily. Hadn't Andy been on the tours in the morning? Hadn't Andy been listening to the talks in the afternoon? Hadn't he learned anything at all? Yet to Hans's credit, the next day he was curious enough to check out Andy's story. The following night he was pale and shaken.

"I'm leaving on the train for Holland as soon as possible, Andrew," he said.

Andy never saw him again.

On Sunday, the thirty thousand visitors were supposed to demonstrate at a huge stadium. Andy went to church instead. In spite of all the oppression of basic rights, the Poland allowed its citizens to practice religion even though the government constantly propagandized against the foolishness of such practices. Andy saw several Catholic churches with their doors open. Finally he found a Reformed Church. The church was about three-quarters full. And the congregation was not just old people. Young people were there, too. They all sang hymns with enthusiasm. Andy could not understand the sermon, but it must have been Bible-based because the preacher constantly waved his Bible. After the service, the preacher, who must have spotted Andy's foreign look, sought him out.

"Welcome," the preacher said in English, as he gathered a bunch of youths around Andy. They peppered him with questions about the West. He peppered them with questions about Polish Communism. They claimed they could worship as long as they stayed away from politics. They took the liberty of directing him to a Baptist church so he could see them worship, too, an invitation that Andy couldn't pass up.

In the Baptist church Andy was asked to come to the podium. No one there spoke English, but one woman spoke German. In the rough German he had acquired, Andy labored through a sermon, and the woman translated his

84

words into Polish. His sermon may have been rough, but it was nevertheless a sermon—indeed, an exposition of the Gospel—behind the Iron Curtain!

As the service ended the pastor had tears in his eyes. He confided, "Even if we could not have understood one word you spoke, just seeing a fellow Christian like yourself means so much to us. At times we feel we are all alone."

In the days ahead Andy made another great discovery. Warsaw was rumored to have a shop that sold Bibles! One morning Andy rushed to an address on New World Street. Sure enough, there in a shop window were Bibles, including red-letter editions and pocket versions. Inside the shop Andy startled the clerk when he asked him if he spoke English. But then the clerk rattled off his wares.

"What are you doing here?" the clerk asked suddenly.

" 'If one member suffer, all the members suffer,' " replied Andy.

"Suffer? Who said anything about suffering?" The clerk refused to acknowledge Andy's quote from First Corinthians. "Surely you don't mean us Poles? We are free people. As you can see we are free to publish and distribute Bibles."

"Of course," said Andy pleasantly. "Are there such Bible stores in the other Communist countries?"

"In some countries, yes. In some countries, no." He looked at Andy shrewdly. "People say—of course I have no way of knowing if they speak the truth—that the Russians are more desperate for Bibles than a pair of American blue jeans. They say a man can smuggle a bag of Bibles into Russia and trade them for a motorcycle. Then he returns, sells the motorcycle, and buys more Bibles. He smuggles these into Russia, too. And on and on goes the smuggling until the man is very rich indeed."

After that odd story Andy excused himself. There was a tension in the shop that he could not fathom. No doubt the man actually sold Bibles, but he acted as if he expected the ax to fall at any moment. Did he tell the story to tip Andy off to a good scheme? Or did he tell it simply because he hated Russians? Andy had heard the Poles despised the Russians, and had for centuries.

In the meantime, Andy had to complete his mission to distribute hundreds of "The Way of Salvation" booklets. He soon tested this Communist regime in Poland to the limit. But he was not a fool. Passing out booklets on a street corner near a traffic policeman was not his idea of brilliant strategy so he haunted bus stops and tram stops. There he was immersed in the milling crowds. After quickly glancing around, people were more than willing to snatch a booklet from his outstretched hand. Then they darted off. If Andy spotted a red-banded military cap working though the crowd, he, too, darted off. But why am I doing that? he asked himself. Who knows soldiers better than I?

He had a strange sensation. It was as if he had uttered the old slogan "Get smart—lose your mind!" before one of his suicidal charges. But no, now he had replaced the commando's bravado with faith in God. Still, he was jittery as he approached a group of soldiers. Yet the closer he got to them, the more the uniforms seemed to calm him. After all, he was an old soldier. He came right out and offered them the booklets. They frowned at him in contempt as they looked him over. Then they must have recognized something in his eyes, something wild and fearless and dangerous. They were cautious, even respectful. They examined the booklets he handed them.

"I'm Dutch," he said in German.

"Dutch?" answered one in German.

The conversation immediately died as an officer approached. The soldiers departed. The officer eyed Andy. He said something in Polish. Andy shrugged and said he spoke only Dutch, English, and German.

"What do you have there?" asked the officer in German.

Andy offered him a booklet and the officer studied it. He seemed slightly shaken. Passersby tensed up as they whisked past. They were sure this foreigner must be in trouble. But Andy and the grim officer talked for two hours. The officer wistfully admitted he was raised a Christian. Andy could tell he was starved for spiritual food, and he gladly provided as much as he could.

Several days later Andy had passed out all his booklets. He had personally attended Catholic, Orthodox, Presbyterian, Baptist, Reformed, and Methodist services. Several times he had been asked to preach to the congregation. He had talked to soldiers and common citizens. The Poles were uneasy at times but very receptive. Andy resolved to do a lot of praying for them. The believers in Poland had so much to overcome.

Andy refused to march in The Parade of Triumph, the grand finale that ended the youth conference. Instead, he sat on a bench watching the youthful Communists parade down the main street of Warsaw. The parade illustrated well the struggle ahead. There were so many Communists. They were so dedicated and so young. They marched eight to a rank. Rank after rank, hundreds, thousands, tens of thousands.

What should the believers in the West do? What could Andy himself do?

The WEC, with all its enthusiasm and dedication, had never sent one missionary behind the Iron Curtain. Andy's Bible lay open in his lap as he watched. Suddenly a breeze fluttered the pages. His eyes fell on the second verse of the third chapter in the Book of Revelation: "Be watchful, and strengthen the things which remain, that are ready to die," he read.

Startled, Andy felt as if God were telling him he must not let these remaining believers die. They must be strengthened. Was this Andy's sign? Was his mission in life to be behind the Iron Curtain? He mulled these issues over on the train back to Holland. The more he thought about it, the more he felt the words in Revelation were his mission.

In Amsterdam he visited the Whetstras in their new brown-brick home. They had a car, too, a great luxury in Holland. It was a bright blue Volkswagen sedan. Andy eagerly told the Whetstras all about his experience in Poland. He invited them to decipher the Bible verse that he had seen while watching the parade. What could the verse in Revelation mean?

"How can I, one small man, strengthen anything?" puzzled Andy.

"Don't you see," said Mrs. Whetstra enthusiastically, "that it is when we are weakest that God can use us the most."

"Yes!" agreed Mr. Whetstra. "Paul said it just that way in First Corinthians: 'God hath chosen the weak things of the world to confound the things which are mighty.' "

But Andy was not convinced.

Back in Sint Pancras Geltje and her husband Arie had a wonderful surprise for Andy. Andy usually slept in the loft with Cornelius but now Geltje wanted him to have the little room off the back of the house. Except for when Bas had been so sick, that room had always been the bedroom of Mama and Papa. But a new room had been added onto the house for Papa. Still, it seemed to Andy that the old bedroom should have gone to Geltje and her husband.

"Why me?" he mumbled in embarrassment.

"We know you can't do your important work up in the loft. You need room to work on your papers."

"My papers?" Andy felt worse by the minute. His "work"?

"THIS ARRANGEMENT IS JUST UNTIL YOU GET MARRIED AND GET YOUR OWN HOUSE!" It was Papa. His thundering remark broke the tension.

But Andy was humbled. Everyone was so helpful, so eager to defer their own interests for his. Didn't they know how confused he was? Moreover, the concern his own family showed him was shared by others. Everyone wanted to know about Poland. What was Communism really like? Church groups, schools, and civic groups in the vicinity asked him to speak. Andy accepted every invitation. He wasn't sure what God wanted him to do. But maybe his next move would develop out of all this exposure. Soon he was speaking to groups as far away as Amsterdam and Haarlem. He was uneasy because everyone acted as if he had some definite mission and he really had none, not even a source of income. But he kept telling himself his unease over money was trifling because the WEC school had taught him to trust God and not worry about money.

Once when he began to speak to a church group in Haarlem he recognized some people who had been in Warsaw. They were Communists. He expected them to heckle him but he was pleasantly surprised. They said nothing, even though he dwelled on the hidden eyesores of Warsaw. But the Communists approached him after the meeting. A woman he remembered as one of the leaders of the Holland delegation to Poland confronted him.

"I didn't like your talk," she said bluntly.

"I didn't think you would."

"You were there only three weeks. Yet you presume to be some kind of expert."

"I only describe what I actually saw."

"That's just it. You didn't see enough." She waited for Andy to respond. He said nothing. "I am in charge of picking fifteen people from Holland to go to Czechoslovakia. The trip will last four weeks. I am inviting you to be one of the fifteen."

"But I can't afford it."

The woman studied him. Was Andy bluffing? She called his bluff. "I'll find a way to pay for your trip."

"Good. I'll go."

seven

November can be a dreary time of year in eastern
Europe. But Prague, the capital city of Czechoslovakia, depressed Andy for reasons other than the dismal weather. This tour group was much smaller than the
one in Poland. He could not slip away in all the confusion
as he had there. Every day after the carefully orchestrated
tours and speeches, his Communist hostess would look at
him as if to say, "Well, surely now you see the real
Communism, don't you?"

The tour was almost over when Andy got his opening.
Their guide mentioned as evidence of Czechoslovakia's
religious freedom a group of Bible scholars who had just
recently translated the Bible into modern Czech. They
were also working on a Bible dictionary. "Oh, I would like
to visit these scholars!" said Andy.

Remarkably, he was taken to see them that afternoon.
His Dutch companions did not go, an indication of the

contempt most western Communists had for the Bible. They considered it nothing; to them it was a worthless book. Andy suspected the hardcore Communists of the eastern European countries and Russia were frightened by the power of the Bible. That was why they suppressed it. Yet here in Czechoslovakia a group was supposedly allowed to do Bible studies. Was it true? Right in the heart of the capital city Prague was a large building called the Interchurch Center. Andy's guide explained it was the center for all the Protestant churches in the country. The great size of the facility was astonishing. In a suite of offices were scholars with desks stacked with paper. It was a very impressive display.

"Could I see the new translation?" asked Andy, expecting to see a nicely bound Bible in the Czech language.

"Of course," said his guide.

Soon one scholar brought forth a massive, much-handled bundle of typed pages. Andy was startled. "Oh, you have not published it yet?" he asked in German.

"It's been ready since the war ended," answered the scholar defensively.

"Very impressive," Andy told his guide, who was getting alarmed.

"What about the Bible dictionary?"

"It's almost ready, too," answered the guide.

"But what good will it do to have a dictionary with no Bible?" Andy shot back.

One of the scholars grumbled, "It's very difficult to find Bibles here nowadays."

The guide was looking uncomfortable. This was not good. All this jabbering back and forth in German was hard to follow. The guide's specialty was English. Suddenly the guide told Andy the visit was over. They must get back to the rest of the group.

"I gained some real insight there," Andy said truthfully.

He had seen the degree to which Communists will deceive. The Interchurch Center was all an illusion. No concrete results were permitted. But to further their deception about freedoms allowed under Communism, they maintained this extravagant front. The next day Andy asked the guide to take him to what was nominally a religious bookstore. At first sight it, too, was impressive. The shelves were well supplied with books that seemed to have religious content. Also there were statues, pictures, records, sheet music, stationery, and crosses.

Andy asked the sales clerk politely in German, "Could you please show me a red-letter edition of the Bible?"

"They are out of stock right now, sir."

"Oh, they must be popular. Well, how about a regular black and white Bible?"

"They are out of stock too, sir."

"So you have no Bibles to sell?"

With what must have been a nod of approval from the guide, the sales clerk disappeared into a back room. Soon she reappeared with something in a brown sack. "I found what you wanted, sir," she said, smiling apologetically. "You see, few Bibles in Czech are being printed right now. Not many people want the old translation. It's outdated. But here is a copy." She added brightly, "We are all waiting for the wonderful new translation."

"I expect you will wait forever," commented Andy in Dutch, all the while smiling.

Andy had found out what he needed to know about the new Bibles. They were unavailable. He had one more goal for his trip: He wanted to see a church service. Knowing this tour would not permit such an excursion, Andy planned his escape. He had observed that the rear sliding door of their tour bus was faulty. A gap of one foot remained even when the door was supposedly closed. So on Sunday morning— the last day of the tour—as they rumbled around Prague, he waited for his chance. At one stop, as the guide in the front of the bus expounded on some heroic act by a Communist, he slipped outside. He watched gratefully as smoke spewed from the exhaust pipe and the bus roared off.

A short time later he was inside a church. Some worshipers carried hymnals and most carried loose-leaf notebooks. After the service began Andy could plainly see the loose-leaf notebooks were makeshift hymnals. Only a very few carried Bibles. When the preacher referred to a certain passage, Andy could see people surge toward the few who had Bibles in an effort to read the precious words. *How these children of the church must crave a Bible,* Andy thought. He could get the sacred text anytime he wanted it in Holland. He could own a hundred Bibles if he wished, even a thousand. Here there seemed a thousand people for every Bible.

After the service Andy approached the pastor. "I am from Holland," he said, introducing himself.

The pastor was stunned. "I heard we were opening up our borders, but I didn't believe it. There is little you can believe from the government here. Please come with me to my apartment."

There, in the privacy of his home, the pastor poured

his heart out to Andy. The Communist government was slowly strangling the church. Every two months a minister had to renew his license. Any minister who asserted Christianity too strongly was denied renewal. Every sermon had to be written out and approved before it could be delivered to the congregation. The Communists even selected the divinity students. It was just a matter of time before the church died.

"They seem to have a million ways to deceive people," commented Andy.

"It is almost time for the second service. Will you come and speak to us?"

Andy was stunned. "Can I really preach here?"

"You are not going to preach," said the minister slyly. "You are bringing us 'greetings' from our friends in Holland. After that you might bring us 'greetings' from the Lord."

Through an interpreter Andy offered a greeting from Holland, which took a couple of minutes. His greeting from Jesus Christ, however, lasted half an hour. The congregation seemed thrilled. It must have been the first real sermon they had heard in a long time. Soon the minister and the interpreter were shuttling Andy to other churches. That day he brought "greetings" to five churches! It was evening when he reached the last of the five, a Moravian church. He tried not to think about what the Communists in his tour group were doing at that moment. He was sure they were furious.

The congregation in the Moravian church numbered over a hundred. Andy was heartened to see almost half of them ranged in age from eighteen to twenty-five. This particular church was not dying—not yet. After he had delivered his greeting the youths gathered around him, flooding him with questions. They couldn't believe Christians in Holland got good jobs. They were amazed believers were allowed into the good universities. It was a fact of life with them that to practice Christianity meant second-class citizenship and suffering. One youth stepped forward and gave Andy a silver lapel ornament shaped like a tiny cup. Andy now noticed several youths were wearing the tiny cup.

"Take this with you," said one youth passionately.

Andy's interpreter explained. "When the Dutch people ask you about this small cup tell them about the Czech Christians. Remind them we are part of the Body of Christ, too. Tell them we are in pain. That is why we call this pin the 'Cup of Suffering.' "

Andy was humbled by these visits to churches. How many Christians in the West would suffer like this for Christ? But he had to pull himself together. He had been away from his tour group all day. When he arrived back at the hotel, members of the group were not there. They were having their farewell banquet somewhere, Andy supposed. He walked over to a restaurant where they had eaten a number of times. They were not there—but the tour director was!

Her face was volcanic, though at first she was too angry to speak. "I called every hospital, every police station. Finally I called the morgue. Unhappily for me, you were not there! Where were you?" she asked outraged.

Andy put on his best dumb Dutchman look. "Somehow we got separated. I just walked around. I hope I didn't inconvenience you."

"If I have any influence, Mister van der Bijl, you will never set foot in Czechoslovakia again!"

Andy wondered if perhaps he hadn't pushed too far, too fast. Still, if God wanted him to do this, shouldn't he forge fearlessly ahead? But rubbing authorities the wrong way began to haunt him after he returned to Holland. The trips to Poland and Czechoslovakia had virtually been dropped in his lap. Now months had passed and nothing was happening, even though he tirelessly applied for visas. He assaulted the consulates of every country behind the Iron Curtain: Russia, Czechoslovakia, Romania, Poland, East Germany, Yugoslavia, Hungary, Bulgaria, and even little Albania! Day after day in his room at home he scribbled answers on applications, questionnaires, and forms of every kind, often in triplicate. He drafted sober, non-threatening letters. He felt very much alone at times. He wanted a wife. If only he had a soulmate to share his mission. But who would want to share such a poor life as mine? he wondered.

At least he had a tiny source of income. The Dutch magazine Kracht Van Omhoog had asked him to write a series of articles about his experiences behind the Iron Curtain. Although the magazine offered no payment, its readers saw in Andy a cause that had to be supported. They started sending him money; he had asked for nothing. However, the money relieved his sense of guilt over living off the labors of Geltje and her husband. Finally he could contribute to the household. He replaced his one ragged jacket. He mailed Bibles to various friends he had met in Poland and Czechoslovakia. Perhaps they would never get through, but who could say for sure?

"I must make the effort," Andy said.

Then a peculiar thing happened. Because of his articles in Kracht Van Omhoog, a prayer group in the town of Amersfoort wrote him. Amersfoort was not far from Ermelo, where Ben lived. The letter said the Holy Spirit had instructed them to write Andy. They had no idea why. Could he come and talk to them? Andy was excited. If true, this was really God at work. So he went to Amersfoort.

The prayer group of about a dozen met in the home of Karl de Graaf, a builder of dikes. This prayer group was like none Andy had witnessed. They had no structure whatsoever. They simply prayed as if they had run up their antennae to await inspiration. Occasionally someone would pray out loud. Usually the prayer was joyous praise of God. They were a very happy group. Andy saw the occasional spoken prayer as love just suddenly bubbling up! Occasionally someone might pray aloud some information or instruction. Andy was so absorbed in the experience he was amazed to learn it was four-thirty in the morning when the de Graafs led him to their guest bedroom. Yet nothing transpired during his visit to Amersfoort that directly affected Andy. He went back to Sint Pancras perplexed.

Several days later Karl de Graaf came to Andy's home in Sint Pancras. He asked, "Andy, do you know how to drive?"

"Do I know how to drive. . .?"

"A car!"

"No, I don't."

"Last night in our prayer meeting we had a word from the Lord about you. You need to learn how to drive."

"But I'll never own a car!"

"Andy," said Karl with a pained look, "we are only

passing on the message of the Holy Spirit."

Andy did nothing about it. Passing the driver's test in Holland was notoriously difficult. It was hardly the thing one wanted to attempt when one did not have any hope of ever owning a car. Andy might as well have practiced brain surgery! Besides, Andy was writing more magazine articles. He still had many forms to fill out and letters to write. He could not flag in his obligation to get back into the Iron Curtain countries. Any Iron Curtain country!

A week later Karl de Graaf was at the door again. "How are the driving lessons coming?"

"Listen, Karl, about those—"

"I was afraid of that! Come on."

Within moments Andy was behind the steering wheel of Karl de Graaf's car. Karl was a thorough taskmaster. He drilled Andy for days. In only a few weeks Andy passed the difficult driver's test. The absurdity of the whole thing hit Andy as he put his new driver's license into his pocket. He didn't even own a bicycle anymore. "I sold it when I went to England back in 1953," he told Karl de Graaf.

With the fall of 1956 came a major event in eastern Europe as the Hungarians revolted against the Communists. As a result, Russian tanks and troops flooded in to prop up their Communist "puppet" regime. Thousands of Hungarian refugees fled the country. Enormous refugee camps sprang up just outside the Hungarian border in Austria. The camps lacked everything. Many of the Dutch volunteered to take needed supplies to the refugees, and Andy was almost first in line to go. He huddled with other volunteers in the front of the bus. The rest of the bus was crammed with food and clothing. Medicine was taken as well. Andy soon discovered that the huge camps in Austria were holding refugees not only from Hungary but from every Communist country, and especially Yugoslavia. In addition, West Germany had huge camps of refugees from East Germany and Czechoslovakia. Andy and his group quickly depleted their supplies.

"But we can still give them God's Word," volunteered Andy.

Andy held prayer meetings. Refugees from Hungary and Yugoslavia were woefully ignorant of the Bible. With the help of interpreters Andy offered classes in the most elementary Bible instruction. The effect was stunning. Ignorance became faith. Despair changed to hope. Bitterness became love. Andy was particularly struck by an elderly couple from Yugoslavia. Unkempt and dirty, they were the picture of despair. During the first Bible lesson the old man began to weep. Soon they were taking care of themselves. To Andy, it was wonderful to see but heartbreaking, too.

"If only I had known the truth years ago," blurted the old man.

All those years lost! Andy had to do something. He knew the problem, and he also knew the answer. Back in Holland once again, he pursued a visa for Yugoslavia harder than ever. Still, all his paperwork seemed to bring no results. Meanwhile he was off again to collect more supplies for the refugee camps.

Andy was in West Berlin when he received a telegram from Sint Pancras. Papa had dropped dead in his beloved garden. Andy rushed home for the funeral. It was the custom in Holland, at the death of a spouse, to reopen the family grave. As Mama's grave was reopened and Papa's coffin was lowered to rest on top of her coffin, Andy was glad Papa had seen him finally take the straight path. If only Mama had known how her son read the Bible she gave him! But maybe Mama did know. Andy took Papa's new add-on room so Geltje and Arie could have the little bedroom in the house. Moreover, the add-on room had its own entrance so he would not have to disturb the rest of the family with his coming and going. But he wasn't there long.

"I must return to Germany and the camps," he announced to his sister.

Helping at the camps was like going to college to study how to deal with Communist totalitarianism. Andy met refugees from every Communist country. He learned all the ins and outs of each country. He heard how strict their border guards were. He learned about their secret police. He memorized little things about a country that might endear him to strangers there, even officials. He was instructed in their written as well as their unwritten laws. He always asked just how open a Christian could be. He compiled lists of friendly contacts.

A pattern within the Communist nightmare emerged for Andy. Not all countries behind the Iron Curtain were the same. Poland, Czechoslovakia, Yugoslavia, Hungary, and East Germany—the Communist countries adjacent to the free countries of the West—pretended to offer religious freedom but persecuted Christians in subtle ways. They were willing to choke the church to death slowly. On the other hand, the more distant Communist countries—Romania,

Bulgaria, Albania, and Russia itself—made less of a pretense of allowing religious freedom. They wanted the church dead now. *Will I ever dare penetrate those distant regimes?* Andy wondered hopefully.

The camps in West Berlin were old ones. In them were children twelve years old who had never been inside a real house. The sacrament of marriage had almost been obliterated in the camps by a mindless regulation. Two single people received more space and clothing than a married couple. As a result marriage was now rare. Most of the children were illegitimate. Most children were chronically sick, too, with tuberculosis very common. In such a camp of despair Andy needed his morning Quiet Time with God more than ever.

One morning he heard a voice say, "Today you will get a visa for Yugoslavia."

Was it a real voice? Or was it in his thoughts? It was the most mystical thing that had happened to him during Quiet Time. Before, when he felt as if God were talking to him, he expected it. It was a natural result of some prayer or special pleading. But he never thought he heard an actual voice. He could hardly wait for the mail that day.

"Letter for you from Holland," greeted the mail carrier to Andy later in the day.

Geltje had forwarded a letter to Andy. It was from the Yugoslavian embassy in Holland, but the news was not what Andy wanted to hear. The embassy was writing to inform Andy that his visa was denied. This couldn't be. The "voice" had said otherwise. He stormed the Yugoslavian consulate in Berlin and was given material to reapply. He made only one change. Instead of writing down "missionary" for his occupation, he wrote "teacher." That wasn't a falsehood. That was merely doing what Jesus counseled his disciples to do in Matthew 10: ". . .I send you forth as sheep in the midst of wolves: be ye therefore wise as serpents, and harmless as doves." An official at the Yugoslavian consulate processed his new application in twenty minutes.

Andy had his visa! Apparently God knew that Andy had to be prodded.

A second astonishing thing happened the same day. Because Geltje had no phone, Andy telephoned the Whetstras in Amsterdam to tell them he was going to Yugoslavia.

"You had better come and pick up your keys then," said Mr. Whetstra mysteriously.

Andy grumbled about the bad connection. "It sounded like you said keys."

"I did. My wife and I have decided you must use our Volkswagen."

The Volkswagen Beetle! Were the Whetstras volunteering their nice new car? Andy rushed to Amsterdam. It was true, and the Whetstras could not be talked out of it. Had Karl de Graaf talked to them? No, answered the Whetstras. The decision came to them during prayer. Andy was doing important business for the Lord. It was the least they could do. Andy stammered his thanks. And it was not a loan. Mr. Whetstra had transferred the title to him. Andy now owned the car! He was speechless.

He now feverishly planned his trip. He couldn't go to Yugoslavia empty-handed. He scoured Amsterdam for any kind of Christian material in Serbo-Croatian and Slovenian, the Slavic languages spoken by most of the people there. The money to buy material came from Karl de Graaf, who seemed totally unsurprised by Andy's acquisition of a car. As Andy loaded the car, he stowed his camping gear in the trunk. In the back seat of the car he stashed his luggage. The luggage was jammed with tracts and portions of the New Testament. Hidden in every fold and recess of the tent and sleeping bag in the trunk were more of the same.

In March 1957 Andy left Holland, intending to drive his blue Volkswagen Beetle all the way across Europe to the Yugoslav border. What would he find on his next adventure behind the Iron Curtain?

eight

Yugoslavia was six hundred miles from Amsterdam. Driving the blue Volkswagen Beetle through West Germany and then across Austria, Andy finally arrived at the last village in Austria before the border of Yugoslavia. Yugoslavia was a Communist country under a very strong dictator, Marshal Tito. Tito was so strong, Yugoslavia was the one eastern European country that thumbed its nose at Russia. Indeed, the Yugoslavs were a stubborn and defiant people. Getting thrown in jail in Yugoslavia was not a good idea.

Andy prayed what he came to call the "Smuggler's Prayer":

> "Lord, in my luggage I have Scriptures that I
> want to take to Your children across this border.
> When You were on earth, You made blind eyes
> see. Now, I pray, make seeing eyes blind. Do not

let the guards see those things You do not want
them to see."[1]

In 1957, the Communists permitted visitors to bring
into Yugoslavia only items for their own personal use. The
border guards were especially alert for any items in quantity because of the black market, an illegal underground
"market" for trading items brought in from the West.
Printed material was considered doubly dangerous. It
could not only be sold in the black market, but it could also
be used as propaganda against Communism. Printed material in quantity had no chance of passing a border guard's
scrutiny, and of course, Andy's little blue Beetle was brist-
ling with such material! After saying his prayer Andy took
a deep breath and drove to the barrier where border guards
would examine his belongings. His sunniest face greeted
the two guards who came out of booth to process him. One
guard grumpily took his passport and visa.

"Dutch?" said the guard in surprise. The guard spoke
German. That was very good.

"Yes, Dutch," answered Andy in German.

"Pop your trunk, Dutchman!" called the second guard.

The trunk on a VW Beetle was under the front hood.
Andy nervously tried to watch the second guard through
the raised hood in front of him. *Lord, make his eyes blind,*
prayed Andy. But meanwhile, the first guard commanded
Andy to slide his seat forward and pull his luggage out
from the back seat. Andy had hoped to distract the guards
during their inspections. But how could he distract two
guards from their inspections at the same time? Surely they
would find all his printed material and arrest him.

"What do you have to declare?" barked the first guard.

"Money, camera, and a wristwatch," said Andy.

One of his suitcases was lying open now on the ground. The guard pawed through it. Tracts were scattered all through his folded shirts and clothes. This was it. Surely the guard would feel the tracts even if he were blind to them!

Andy couldn't bear to watch. "Very dry for this time of year, isn't it?' he said breezily.

"For March?" mulled the guard.

"Not for March," volunteered the second guard. "Our rainy season is during the middle of the summer."

"Really?" said Andy. "In Holland our rainiest months are September and October."

"Our rainiest month is July," said one guard.

"July? I don't think so," said the other guard. "It rains more in August."

Neither guard now had the slightest interest in Andy's belongings. It was lonely on the frontier. Few people came though this border crossing. The guards happily bantered about the weather. Then they asked, pointedly staring at Andy's feet, if the Dutch still wore wooden shoes. "Occasionally," Andy answered laughing. And just how many windmills were there in Holland? "Oh, thousands!" cried Andy. Finally, as an afterthought, one of the guards asked if Andy had anything else to declare.

"Only 'small' things," shrugged Andy.

Andy hadn't lied. All his religious items were rather small. The guards frowned as he left, disappointed to see him leave. Andy was almost disappointed himself. It was such a mystical experience. It was impossible for the guards not to have seen or felt his printed material. And yet they were oblivious to the books and tracts. Truly, nothing is impossible for God, Andy thought. Suddenly, he wanted to make every lost soul behind the Iron Curtain realize that.

Andy drove into Zagreb, a very large city in the province of Slovenia. To illustrate how tenuous his mission was, his only possible contact was a Christian whom the Dutch Bible Society had not heard from in twelve years! Andy actually wrote the man a letter before he left Holland, stating in a vague way that a Dutchman would be arriving in Zagreb at a certain time. Andy had to use a twelve-year-old address. Now in Zagreb he drove to that site. The moment he stepped out of the VW, a man came forward cautiously.

"Are you the Dutchman?" asked the man, eyeing Andy's Dutch license plates.

"Have you ever heard of the Dutch Bible Society?" asked Andy.

The man named someone in the society Andy knew. This man was his contact! "I have not lived at this address for many years," he said, shaking his head, "but somehow the postal service found me to deliver your letter."

As Andy heard so often from Christians behind the Iron Curtain, the man was overjoyed Andy was there. It meant so much to know that Christians on the "outside" cared. The man felt so alone. But the man knew Andy's time was limited by his visa. He had only fifty days to spread the Gospel. The man quickly arranged meetings for Andy with other contacts. He found someone to translate for Andy. Soon Andy drove off with his translator, an engineering student named Nikola.

"Our first stop is a small church not far from Zagreb," said Nikola.

Over the next seven weeks Andy preached at eighty meetings, besides distributing his Christian materials. If one didn't delve into matters deeply, it seemed the Communists did not persecute the church. They allowed Christians to have services. There were no restrictions on Andy preaching. But the Yugoslavian Communists had a definite strategy. They chose to ignore older Christians and persecute the young. The schools hammered constantly that there was no God. Only simple fools believed such nonsense. As a result, most young people avoided church services, even if their parents were strong Christians. The youths did not want to look like fools to their peers. Besides that, any child suspected of being an earnest Christian was thrown out of school! To get back in school the child had to disavow Christianity. The Communists theorized that in a generation or two Christianity would be dead. "All the more reason to get the Gospel out," reflected Andy.

As Andy moved south he realized that the persecution of all Christians became more and more blatant. By the time he reached Macedonia he learned Christians in this area would not go to church before dark. It was not wise to be seen. A typical church night saw peasants coming into church by twos and threes, carrying kerosene lanterns. Even at that the lanterns were turned low so their bearers were in darkness. Andy's only trouble with local police came in Macedonia. As usual, lantern lights pierced the darkness as Christians gathered for the service. But this time two policemen came inside the building and started writing down names. In spite of the intimidation, several answered the altar call to commit themselves to Christ or to reaffirm their commitment.

Andy left, troubled by more than the suspicion the Communists would punish that little church group. Lately he was especially lonely for the companionship of a woman. In fact, he wanted a wife. For several years he had assumed Thile would become his wife. But he had disappointed her, and she had abandoned him. It did no good now even to think about her. Besides, she had married a baker in Gorkum. Andy must not think poorly of her either. She had been an instrument in bringing him to God. "In my evil days she gave me a tinge of a conscience," he admitted.

Yes, Andy now longed for the companionship of a Christian woman. It was true, as the Apostle Paul said, that some men probably should not take a wife. But Paul also grudgingly admitted that some men must marry, and Andy felt he was surely one of those. Yet he often wondered why any woman would want to share his life because there was so much of it that could not be shared. After all, he was committed to spreading the Gospel behind the Iron Curtain. Still, there might be one godly woman back in Holland who wouldn't mind sharing him with the destitute of eastern Europe. He decided that he would pray, and record his requests to the Lord. In the back cover of his Bible he noted that on April 12, 1957, he asked God for a very special favor. "Oh, please, God," he prayed, "give me a wife!"

He drove and drove and preached and preached. The little VW took him through streams. It plowed through mud. It trudged up mountain roads. It rumbled along dry dirt roads. Dust or mud seemed to cover every inch of the car.

At times Andy forgot the little car was blue. But he didn't take the car for granted. Every morning in Quiet Time he prayed for the car. "Lord, please keep our little friend running. I have no money for repairs, nor do I have the time." In meetings Andy told about his faithful little servant. Many laughed and called it the "miracle car."

Cars were such a novelty in Yugoslavia, especially foreign cars, that it was the custom for a driver to stop and talk to any other driver he encountered on a road. On one occasion Andy and Nikola stopped to talk to a truck driver.

The truck driver beamed. "So this is the 'miracle car'!"

"You have heard of us?"

"Oh, yes. Do you mind if I examine your miracle car?"

Andy agreed, although he was suspicious. Was the man just a good-natured Yugoslavian, or was he a Communist who would like nothing more than to expose Andy as a fake? Suppose he found that the miracle car was just another very well-serviced vehicle? The man went around to the rear of the VW to examine the tiny engine.

After a while the man asked, "What service have you provided for this car?"

"I put gas in the tank," answered Andy. "That's all I've done since I left Holland."

"I believe you," said the man. "This is the filthiest engine I've ever seen. The air filter is blocked. The carburetor is gummed up. The spark plugs are completely fouled." He stepped back and laughed, almost hysterically. "This car can't possibly run!"

"And yet it does," piped in Nikola.

"I believe this is truly a miracle car," gushed the man, "but how far can you push a miracle? Please let me service this car for you. I'm a mechanic."

The truck driver followed Andy and the VW into a village where Andy was going to preach that night. While Andy preached and Nikola interpreted, the man broke down the tiny engine and cleaned each part. He rebuilt the carburetor. He put in new filters. He changed the oil. When he had finished he would not accept one penny for his effort. He was humbled to be part of Andy's miraculous mission.

On May 1, 1957, Andy and Nikola drove into Belgrade, the capital of and the largest city in Yugoslavia. May Day was a huge day of celebration in Communist countries. It marked the anniversary of one of the Communists' first successful international gatherings. Belgrade was so crowded Andy and Nikola thought they were resigned to sleeping in the cramped car until a local pastor took them into his home. At his first church service Andy expected the people in this capital city to be more cynical and more aloof than others he had preached to in Yugoslavia. In fact, he expected few would show up.

Yet the congregation of well-dressed cosmopolitans became so swollen the doors had to be taken off their hinges. That way people outside the building could hear better. Even though every word Andy spoke had to be translated into Serbo-Croatian by Nikola, the congregation remained attentive. When Andy made the altar call, it seemed everyone in the building started to surge forward.

"Surely they misunderstood me," he whispered to Nikola. "Ask them to acknowledge the call by holding up their hands instead. But emphasize first the suffering they are inviting at the hands of their government."

Nikola spoke several sentences to them in Serbo-Croatian. All hands went up! And yet when Andy began to explain what steps they needed to take next, including regular church attendance, prayer, and Bible study, a gloom fell over the congregation. Eyes lowered. Shoulders sagged. They were no longer with him. Hope seemed to drain right out of them. What had happened? The pastor explained through Nikola that the people had no Bibles. "No Bibles in a large, cosmopolitan city like Belgrade?" gasped Andy. He had Nikola ask the congregation for a show of hands of those who owned a Bible.

"I count a total of seven," murmured Nikola.

With the help of the pastor, Andy worked out a system of Bible sharing but it was clear from the start that his idea was not going to be very effective. Even later that night he couldn't believe that out of hundreds of anxious, willing people only seven owned Bibles. God could not have told him more clearly if he had written the words across the evening sky that the greatest need for these people behind the Iron Curtain was the sacred Bible. What a weapon for God the Bible would be! And what a comfort to these suffering Christians.

"Yet a Bible is the most difficult thing to smuggle past a border guard," reflected Andy.

Its bulkiness made the tracts seem a cakewalk in comparison. Still, he wanted to believe that his Smuggler's Prayer would blind the border guards to bulky Bibles, too. He must not lose faith. And yet there were other problems. Where would Andy find the Bibles? He had learned during his search for materials for this trip that Bibles in foreign tongues were rare in quantity. He would need thousands to do any good! Otherwise his efforts were just pebbles in an ocean—even though in Yugoslavia he had driven five thousand miles and converted hundreds of Christians.

As he left Yugoslavia he realized he had another 600 miles to pray about it before he reached Sint Pancras. But besides the dilemma of the Bible, again he brooded over his need for a wife. When would his prayer be answered? His loneliness now gnawed at him constantly. Every once in a while his loneliness would just slap him in the face. He was almost thirty years old. Once he flipped his Bible open to Isaiah 54:1 and read a verse that seemed to tell him his children were the desolate, that he would never have any children of his own. He just could not accept that.

"Didn't you say, God, in Genesis, 'It is not good that the man should be alone; I will make him an help meet for him'?" Most men were not complete without a woman. The need was as old as creation.

Now on his way back to Holland he prayed for a wife a second time. Back in Sint Pancras he threw himself into his activity. He preached. He lectured. He wrote articles for *Kracht Van Omhoog*. He waited for inspiration for his next trip. He tried not to think about his craving for a wife. Yet on July 7 he recorded in his Bible again that he prayed for a wife. Three times Paul had asked God to remove the "thorn out of his side." The Bible was silent as to what the thorn actually was. It might have been some kind of ailment. Finally, Paul had to accept it, whatever it was. Paul would not ask a fourth time. That effort suited Andy. He would not ask God a fourth time for a wife. "Either God will answer my three prayers for a wife or not at all!" he concluded.

In September while in his morning Quiet Time an image struck him. Corrie van Dam! Pretty. Pure. Wise beyond her years. She had always been so perfect for Andy. It was just that Andy thought of her as a little sister. How old would she be now? Why, she would be twenty-five! His heart sank. No woman as pretty as Corrie would be single at that age. Still, why had he remembered her with such force? He drove to Alkmaar. If he had maintained his friendships the way he should, he would have known if she were married. But on the other hand, he couldn't forget that ever since he returned from Scotland he had been constantly busy. He had gone to Poland and never stopped running since. He had filled out hundreds of forms, written hundreds of letters, and visited contacts.

His heart was in his mouth when he knocked at the door of the house where he had enjoyed coffee and cookies so many times. But he sickened when the door opened to reveal a strange face. He learned the van Dams had moved to a small apartment. Undoubtedly Corrie didn't live with her parents any longer. Yet he rushed to the new address, ignoring all common sense. He knocked on the door of the small apartment with little hope of seeing Corrie.

As if in answer to his prayer, Corrie answered the door. "Andy van der Bijl!" she cried.

"Why, you're still at home," he blurted in return.

Her face sobered. "Actually, I live in Haarlem, Andy. I'm in my final year of nursing school. I'm home because Father is sick." She added gloomily, "Very sick."

She was in a crisp, white nurse's uniform. Andy saw no wedding ring on her finger. He was full of hope now. How her face had brightened when she first opened the door!

115

Surely she felt some affection for him. But he brushed aside those thoughts when Mrs. Van Dam appeared. She seemed already in mourning. He learned Mr. van Dam was in a back bedroom. Andy's reunion with Corrie had become a somber occasion. He went back and talked to the ailing Mr. van Dam while Corrie busied herself with nursing duties.

Over the next few weeks he visited the van Dams often. But in October he was informed his visa to Hungary was approved. He knew he should propose to Corrie before he left, but it was impossible when her father was dying. Then Mr. van Dam passed away. Andy certainly couldn't propose to Corrie while she was grieving either! Meanwhile he scoured Amsterdam for Christian material in the Hungarian language which he then stockpiled. When he spoke to groups now in Holland about his visits behind the Iron Curtain, he said nothing about smuggling religious material into the Communist countries. He must protect his activity as well as his contacts in those countries. What he was doing put more people at risk with every passing year. As the day to leave for Hungary approached, he grew more and more apprehensive about Corrie, too. He knew he must propose to her before he left. But what if she refused? It was obvious to him that as pretty as she was, she had had proposals before, proposals she had turned down. Why should I think I'm so special? he asked himself, his confidence lagging.

Yet Corrie was coming out of her grief and their outings were more light-hearted. Andy hoped she loved him as much as he loved her. But so much remained unsaid. What if she were just being kind to an old friend? He had very good memories of Corrie at the factory and the youth meetings. Somehow now he seemed to be putting all those good memories at risk. What if she weren't interested in him in the same way he was interested in her?

Finally, one night when they were riding bikes along the canal he blurted it out. "Corrie, I want you to marry me."

Without pause he went on to tell her that he didn't merely work in the refugee camps. Nor did he merely enter Communist countries to lend support to the churches there. No, he was a smuggler! Did she know how hard her life would be with a husband who slipped forbidden material into Communist countries? He might just disappear one day. It was possible no one in the West would ever know what happened to him. As he talked on and on to Corrie, more and more he realized what a miserable future he did offer her.

His argument was so compelling he finished his proposal by saying, "Don't decide tonight. Tell me your answer when I get back from Hungary."

He left her that night, never having given her a chance to respond. Leaving Holland, he wondered if he had lost his mind. He had intended to get a commitment from Corrie. Instead, he had condemned himself.

nine

When Andy left for Hungary he was hopeful God would let him marry Corrie. But that hope soon became a double-edged sword.

Even though the land route to Hungary through Europe was familiar now to Andy, he had never felt so apprehensive. He approached the Hungarian border with fear and trembling. He felt his faith tested to the limit. Now he had a lot at stake. What if he were thrown in jail for several years? Could he expect Corrie to wait? Perhaps I will never know what she decided, he realized with horror. Yet the border crossing passed without incident. Once again the guards were blind to the religious booklets and tracts stowed in every nook and cranny of the blue VW Beetle. Following the tension of those moments, his descent from the mountainous terrain of Austria into the fertile river plains of Hungary seemed like paradise. Hungary was the southern counterpart of the lush green

119

plains of northern Europe. He drove along the Danube River almost enchanted.

He found that in Hungary, as in other Communist countries, Christianity was often unaccountably tolerated. Consequently, he became bolder and bolder. He developed the art of preaching to officials—but not to border guards!—in long breathless sentences as he answered their questions. The practice was very dangerous, but he felt compelled to do it. It was as if God urged him on. Yet it seemed an old art for him, one born of fighting evil. After all, he had matched wits with the Nazis when he was just twelve years old!

For example, to a question about a religious tract he might say, "It is a tract that tells Communists about Jesus Christ, because Communists can certainly believe in Him, and even as they most certainly love their parents, they can love the Lord Jesus who came to this world because God loved the world and sent His Son in the flesh to save mankind from sin and death, for all people who believe in Jesus Christ shall have eternal life. . ."

"Stop!" fumed many an official after realizing Andy had just delivered a sermonette.

After Andy arrived in the capital city of Budapest, he saw evidence of the recent battles between Russian Communists and the Hungarian rebels they had defeated. He wasn't shocked. Bullet holes and shell craters were old familiar scars of war to Andy. He looked up his contact who was a professor at a distinguished school, and the professor became his interpreter. When Andy saw how the professor's face lit up when he saw brand-new Bibles among Andy's religious material, he knew his mission was blessed.

Andy learned that in the schools a student could win a much-prized citizenship award by avowing the proper attitude toward the so-called superstitions of Christianity. The proper attitude was to scoff at miracles, original sin, fallen man, Christ as God, and other Biblical truths. The church in Hungary was suppressed in just the way Andy expected. Pastors had to get their licenses renewed every two months. Those who preached the true Gospel were refused new licenses. Those who preached anyway went to prison. The professor told Andy that the most successful way to preach the Gospel in Hungary was at weddings and funerals.

"The Communists ignore these rites," explained the professor, shrugging his shoulders.

Nevertheless, after Andy preached at several weddings the police made it clear they suspected him of evangelizing. The alarmed professor arranged for him to visit some contacts in eastern Hungary. When Andy returned to Budapest, the professor had been fired from his job. In spite of that setback, the professor urged Andy to keep up his mission. Yes, some of Andy's contacts in the Communist world would surely suffer. But was anyone risking more than Andy himself? It was the duty of a Christian to stand up for Christ.

Buoyed by the professor's courage, Andy left Hungary for Holland. As he neared Haarlem, where he would see Corrie, his heart was pounding. His head said she would be a fool to share such a life as his. But his heart ached for her hand in marriage. She gave him a pragmatic answer.

"Even if we don't marry, I will miss you and I will worry about your safety and I will pray for you. . ."

"Does that mean 'yes'?"

121

"Yes."

Their wedding in Alkmaar on June 27, 1958, was attended by many family members and friends. Uncle Hoppy came from England. Other old friends from the WEC came, too. Andy also had made many new friends among the workers in the refugee camps. Also present were Corrie's friends from the youth meetings and the medical community. For the honeymoon, Andy borrowed Karl de Graaf's small house trailer. All the wedding guests believed the two would be touring France. But Andy drove no more than a few miles south of Alkmaar into a wooded area for campers. There he and Corrie spent a very loving honeymoon, undisturbed.

Home life was hardly what Andy would have wished for Corrie. The old family home in Sint Pancras was bursting at the seams. Geltje and her husband now had two children. Although Maartje had married and moved away, Cornelius had married and lived in the loft with his wife. Andy and Corrie now lived in the room added on for Papa. The add-on was no more than a small room with a bed, with no plumbing. To make matters worse, Andy was soliciting donations of clothing for the refugee camps, and into the small room in the small house flooded bundles of clothes. At one time eight tons of clothing clogged the house!

That fall, Andy and Corrie made a dent in the mountain of clothing by loading some into the VW and delivering the bundles to the camps. While they remained to work at several camps, Andy applied for a visa to East Germany. Of the Communist countries nearest the West—Poland, Czechoslovakia, Yugoslavia, Hungary, and East Germany—only East Germany remained for him to visit. When his visa was approved he tried to get Corrie to return to Holland, but she refused.

"There is too much work to do here in the camps," she explained.

So Andy found himself leaving her in West Berlin and driving through the Brandenburg Gate into East Germany. East Germany showed Andy yet another face of Communism. Of all the Communist countries he had visited, only East Germany allowed abundant Bibles to be sold. Perhaps Communist officials there realized it was just too easy to get Bibles in German from West Germany. Or perhaps it simply was a tactic of distraction in their overall strategy to squelch Christianity. Their strategy was diabolical. In East Germany the church doors were open, the pastors unhindered.

But how can this be? wondered Andy.

He soon found out. The Communist state allowed religious "freedom" but relentlessly attacked not only Christianity but God. Mottoes were posted everywhere that indicated only a moron would believe in God. Those Christian rites that were deeply woven into the fabric of the old Germany were ridiculed by the new Communist state. The state had mock weddings, a mock baptismal rite called the "welcoming service," and even a mock confirmation rite called "youth consecration." In each official state ceremony a person vowed his loyalty not to God but to the Communist state. With the state relentlessly ridiculing God in the public arena and yet apparently offering all the old rites Germans loved so much, most young East Germans had to wonder of what use was religion.

At one church where Andy preached, he encountered

self-pity. "It's easy for you to speak about mission work," whined the pastor. "You slip in and out, but we must stay here."

Andy nearly lost his temper. "You are already in the mission field. There are millions of Germans here who need to be converted. Why, there are half a million Russian soldiers here to convert! Don't you remember what Paul did in the Greek town of Philippi? The story is told in the Book of Acts." Excited, he read aloud Acts 16:25–34, which began as Paul and Silas were in prison:

> And at midnight Paul and Silas prayed, and sang praises unto God: and the prisoners heard them. And suddenly there was a great earth-quake, so that the foundations of the prison were shaken: and immediately all the doors were opened, and every one's bands were loosed. And the keeper of the prison awaking out of his sleep, and seeing the prison doors open, he drew out his sword, and would have killed himself, sup-posing that the prisoners had been fled.
>
> But Paul cried with a loud voice, saying, "Do thyself no harm: for we are all here."
>
> Then he called for a light, and sprang in, and came trembling, and fell down before Paul and Silas, and brought them out, and said, "Sirs, what must I do to be saved?"
>
> And they said, "Believe on the Lord Jesus Christ, and thou shalt be saved, and thy house."
>
> And they spake unto him the word of the Lord, and to all that were in his house. And

he took them the same hour of the night, and washed their stripes; and was baptized, he and all his, straightway. And when he had brought them into his house, he set meat before them, and rejoiced, believing in God with all his house.

"Paul actually converted his jailers!" boomed Andy in conclusion. The story had its desired effect.

When Andy returned to the refugee camps in West Berlin, he found Corrie underweight with a sickly complexion. Andy was sure she was working herself to death. He had to get her out of there, and he had two choices. He could send her back to Holland. Or he could take her with him on his next trip. He decided to take her with him to Yugoslavia. They loaded the VW with religious literature and left. Yugoslavia was a revelation. Never had he experienced such an easy time getting past guards and officials. Andy realized a missionary team of one man and one woman was a powerful new tool. "It seems the authorities simply did not suspect a man and wife of any mischief," he said with glee.

In Zagreb Andy reunited with old friends, including his interpreter Nikola. Once again, though, he discovered that those who helped him were often punished after he left. Nikola had been dragged into court and fined the equivalent of fifty dollars for translating for Andy. His future as an engineering student was precarious. Nevertheless, he insisted on interpreting for Andy again. But this venture in Yugoslavia was short-lived once Andy started preaching. Within a week he and Corrie were ordered to leave the country as the angry official hammered their passports with ugly red stamps. Andy was sure he was now banned there as he had been banned from Czechoslovakia. He had not stopped applying for another visa to Czechoslovakia, and the government had not stopped rejecting his applications.

Good news came when Andy and Corrie reached West Berlin and discovered that Andy's applications to Romania and Bulgaria had been approved. Andy was stunned. This would be his first venture beyond the tier of the five Communist countries nearest the West. What an adventure that would be! But his joy was blunted by Corrie's worsening physical condition, as she seemed sick all the time now. He rushed her back to Holland. It was November. The doctor came to examine her at the family home in Sint Pancras.

"What is it? A virus?" asked Andy anxiously after the doctor had examined her. "When will she get over this?"

"Don't you know?" The doctor gawked at Andy with surprise. "In June you're going to be a father. Congratulations." Then he added, "Please remove all these bundles of clothing, so your poor wife can get the rest she needs."

Andy rushed to Corrie to tell her how delighted he was. To think that he had come so far. Soon he would be a father. She had completed his life. He would stay and make Corrie as comfortable as possible. But after Andy removed the bundles of clothing to another place he began to calculate. June? That meant he had time to make another trip before the baby came. Corrie saw how restless he was and she urged him to go. A restless, unhappy Andy made everyone else restless and unhappy.

But traveling to Bulgaria and Romania was quite

different from traveling to the countries he had already visited. Bulgaria and Romania were deep behind the Iron curtain. The only practical route to Romania was through Hungary. The only practical route to Bulgaria was through Yugoslavia. Otherwise, one had to travel the length of Italy, take a ship to Greece, and then drive all the way across Greece to enter Bulgaria from the south! Andy had never taken a trip that extensive, or that expensive. Yet he had just recently been thrown out of both Hungary and Yugoslavia. Those nasty red stamps on his passport would probably get him rejected at the borders. He had to get a new passport. On the excuse that all the pages of his passport had been filled with stamps, he applied for a new one, as well as for visas. He was not that surprised when the visa to Yugoslavia was approved. Communist countries were known for their bureaucratic bungling.

"The left five thumbs seldom know what the right five thumbs are doing," cackled those who knew.

With a new passport, his necessary visas, and a carload of religious material in Bulgarian and Romanian, including Bibles, Andy finally took off. He blazed across Europe to enter Yugoslavia. He stopped to see his old friends in Zagreb who gave him some contacts in southern Yugoslavia. Occasionally stopping to visit with these contacts, he worked his way across Yugoslavia. Within fifty miles of the Bulgarian border he was stopped. Officials had discovered he was an undesirable person who was not supposed to be in Yugoslavia.

"You must leave Yugoslavia," insisted an official.

"Fine. I understand completely. In a few hours I will be entering Bulgaria."

"No. You must leave Yugoslavia at Trieste."

Trieste! That was all the way back to the northern border! He hadn't even entered at Trieste. The official was simply making life as difficult as he could for Andy. Andy could not believe his ears. It would have been better if he had never entered Yugoslavia. Why did he stop in Zagreb? Why did he stop to visit along the way? He wanted to step out of his car and stomp and scream. Instead, he smiled and turned the VW around. But he received a parting gift as the official hammered his passport again with ugly red stamps. Another passport tainted! Would it cause him trouble in Bulgaria? Angry and frustrated, Andy knew there was no point even entertaining the thought of making a run for the Bulgarian border. He grew ever more depressed as he backtracked through Yugoslavia. I've got to be back in Holland before June, he reminded himself.

Ironically, Italy's freedom and prosperity drove him to tears. The roads were clogged with traffic. Never had he driven so slow. Six hundred miles of congestion enraged him. Andy felt like he seldom got his little stick-shift VW out of low gear.

Halfway down the boot of Italy his back, which hurt most of the time anyway, began to spasm. By the time he got to Brindisi where the VW would be ferried to Greece, he walked bent forward grotesquely. He was a mental wreck, too. Corrie's birthday—March 31—had come and gone. "She is only two months away from giving birth and I am not even close to Bulgaria!" he cried.

At least the roads in Greece were not congested. But they presented Andy with a different problem. They were about as smooth as a mountain trail. In fact, much of the journey was through mountains. And to think he had two hundred miles of this nightmarish journey before he reached the Greek town of Serrai, where he would enter Bulgaria! When his back was not nagging him, his doubts were. This journey was his worst yet. It seemed destined to fail. And he felt guilty because it looked more and more as if he would miss the birth of his first child.

Then at Serrai he was dealt yet another blow. "Only diplomats are allowed to enter here," he was told. "You can't enter Bulgaria at all from Greece!"

Andy was stunned. "But where do I enter?"

"You must go on to Turkey."

Turkey! Turkey was two hundred spine-rattling miles to the east. Andy stumbled back to his overworked VW. He could not stand upright. Each day was worse. He was being brought to his knees by Communist roadblocks this time! On rocky terrain near the Greek town of Kavalla he spotted a sign in Greek and Latin. The Latin said Filippi! Was that the Philippi of the Bible? Of course! Andy slammed on the brakes. He vaulted out of the VW. He was ecstatic. Imagine! He was seeing the Philippi where Paul was imprisoned. "What a gift! This is a place of miracles!"

Andy drank in the surrounding marble columns and crumbled walls. It was near this very spot that Paul converted Lydia, the "seller of purple," who was considered the first European converted to Christianity. She had invited Paul to her home to preach them the Gospel. Her home, though it no longer stood, could be considered the first church in Europe. Somewhere close to where Andy was standing was where Paul and Silas were flogged and thrown into prison, the prison where God had worked His miracles. Somewhere close to where Andy was standing Paul had stood and demanded justice as a Roman citizen.

"Oh Lord, what a holy place this is," Andy murmured.

Another thing struck him. This was the very spot he had lectured the East Germans about! They had been wallowing in self-pity, just as Andy had been for several days. But Andy's only problems were some lost time and his bad back. At that moment he was buoyed. His back pain lessened; he could stand straighter. He felt like skipping back to the VW.

Hope had returned. Yes, he might miss the birth of his child, but God knew all that ahead of time. God had created the child just as God created Andy. Who was Andy to question this important mission to the God-starved people of Bulgaria? He rushed on. In Turkey he entered Bulgaria with no problem. At the capital city of Sofia he found his contact, a man named Petroff. Petroff explained that all the churches with open doors were puppet churches, or phonies. They did not preach the Gospel. Petroff escorted Andy to one underground church after another. At each church Andy participated in the service, before presenting the congregation with a gift.

"A Bible!" the worshipers would gasp. The Bulgarians were ecstatic. Tears rolled down their cheeks. They were in desperate need of Bibles. Once upon a time, godless Communists had liked to use the thin paper of Bibles to roll their cigarettes. But not these days. Bibles were virtually nonexistent.

"Our government will not allow the printing of Bibles," explained Petroff.

Finally, Andy had distributed all his material written in

Bulgarian, and it was time to drive north to Romania. But the people of Bulgaria begged him to stay. "We have waited years for this. Please stay and preach to us," they pleaded. Never had Andy witnessed such spiritual hunger. How could he have ever doubted the importance of this mission? It was heartbreaking to leave these people behind.

Andy expected Romania to be similar to Bulgaria, but he soon knew he was wrong. Romania was the most severe police state he had entered yet. He had to have his agenda fully outlined and approved by officials. No exceptions were allowed. They must know where he was at every moment. Police were everywhere, even in the tiniest villages. They constantly stopped people in cars and on the street to check their papers. How could Andy ever hope to meet another Christian? How will I ever unravel this mystery of a country? he complained to himself.

Andy slowly figured out what was happening. The church in Romania had been crippled by consolidation. If a church could not fill to capacity, its congregation was assigned to another church. The building was quickly confiscated by the state. By this insidious technique, the government had reduced the number of physical facilities to only a few in the larger cities.

After many false starts, Andy finally found a Christian interpreter just before he was due to leave the country. He had to leave his material with the interpreter and the few Christians he had met. They would have to see that it was distributed. That may have been better anyway. There were many traps in Romania for someone who didn't know the ins and outs of the country's politics. Besides, a blessed event occupied more and more of Andy's thoughts.

"Maybe there is still time!" he said aloud, his eyes sparkling, his hands eagerly gripping the steering wheel. The tiny car careened back to Holland over the long arduous route that had taken him to Romania.

ten

I'm not too late!" Andy cried excitedly when he saw Corrie.

Corrie was larger than he had ever seen her. Thankfully, he had arrived in Holland before Corrie was ready to deliver. And just days later he paced the floor as Corrie gave birth to their baby boy, Joppie. With the arrival of Joppie the family home at Sint Pancras had reached the bursting point. Geltje was expecting her third child and Cornelius's wife was expecting their first. Three families of six adults and five children? Someone had to go. Andy felt it had to be his family. After all, he was trying to run his mission from the home, too.

But he had no money of his own. Even the clothing he and Corrie—and Joppie, for that matter—wore was from the bundles donated for the refugee camps. How would he ever afford an apartment? But an old benefactor came to his rescue again, loaning him money not for an apartment but for a house in Sint Pancras! After thanking Mr. Whetstra once again, Andy considered his new home. The house was rundown and would require much repair, but it was a vast improvement over the tiny add-on.

Just one year later, in 1960, Mark Peter was born. That same year Andy finally made it back into Czechoslovakia. But 1960 stood out for another reason. Andy made his first trip into Russia. He was now publicly going by the name Brother Andrew. It was a habit he picked up from friends in the Communist countries. A person was much harder to track down if the police did not know his last name.

Brother Andrew did not drive into Russia in his VW. This time he had an opportunity to accompany a youth group, much like the one he had accompanied into the Poland back in 1955 on his very first visit behind the Iron Curtain.

"Russia is a strict police state, like Romania," observed Brother Andrew immediately. Indeed, police and soldiers seemed everywhere as authorities tried to monitor every movement of the population. Gloom was the prevailing atmosphere. Eye contact was almost nonexistent.

The religious situation was handled much as it had been in Romania, with the Russians consolidating most churches out of existence. In fact, a sprawling metropolis like Moscow had just one Protestant church. When Brother Andrew attended a service there, the church was packed tightly with two thousand worshippers. Many could not get inside. Because Andrew was a foreigner, he was taken into the balcony. From above he saw how they had to pass offerings—paper currency—overhead and to the front. Their prayer requests were on paper they folded and planed to the front! Andrew learned that the next nearest

Protestant church to Moscow was one hundred miles away. He also learned Bibles were just as rare in Russia as they were in Romania. Afterward Brother Andrew deemed his scouting trip to Russia a success. He had confirmed Russia's need for Bibles.

But the Communist world was often unpredictable. Such a great number of East Germans fled into the freedom offered by West Berlin that in 1961 the Communist government decided they must do something. Almost overnight thousands of soldiers and workers threw up a wall of wire. They furiously labored to make it permanent. Soon a wall of brick, stone, and concrete divided West Berlin from East Berlin. And what a wall! It was twelve feet high and twenty-eight miles long. To further prevent escape, the ends of the wall were extended so that the wall ran for 103 miles. Only two checkpoints or border crossings broke the wall. One remained at the Brandenburg Gate. Andrew was amazed at such a heavy-handed and revealing act done by the Communists out of desperation. "Yet it also reveals that cold, hard-headed Communist hard-liners are still in control behind the Iron Curtain," he observed.

The year 1961 saw the arrival of Andy and Corrie's third son, Paul Denis. Brother Andrew, at the prodding of Corrie, also decided to expand his operations. Driving fifty thousand miles a year had finally worn out the little blue VW Beetle, so he purchased an Opel station wagon that offered much more storage space. But, more importantly, Andrew decided to recruit people to help him. For six years he had steadfastly refused to involve others in his smuggling activities. When he finally relented, his first recruit was Hans Gruber, a hulking six-foot, seven-inch

Dutchman. If Hans weren't easy enough to spot already, he was also exceedingly clumsy. But as a preacher he was spellbinding, and his faith in God rivaled Brother Andrew's. Perhaps cynics would have said he was as reckless as Brother Andrew.

Their first trip together was to Russia. Hans would spell Andrew at the wheel, although Hans was not a very good driver. But Andrew knew he had the right person when Hans kept adding Russian and Ukrainian Bibles to the Opel until it couldn't hold another item. This was no small task: Because of the large Cyrillic script of the Russian language, Russian and Ukrainian Bibles were huge.

Going to Russia by car was running a gauntlet of Communist officials. First, they had to drive through East Germany, and then through Poland. Finally, one hundred miles east of Warsaw they stopped at the Russian border. Beyond was the Russian town of Brest. Andrew and Hans had agreed that at border crossings one would do the talking while the other prayed nonstop. This time it was Hans who spoke his rough Russian to the guards. Andrew prayed, and to his delight the border guards were more interested in cars than smugglers. They barely glanced at the interior of the Opel.

"How many cylinders?" asked one of the guards, who had barely been able to wait to pop up the hood.

Greatly relieved, Andrew and Hans drove into Russia after the border guards got their fill of the shiny Opel engine. Moscow, their destination, was six hundred miles away. There they were assigned to a campground where they pitched a tent. Then they drove into the one Protestant church in Moscow to see Andrew's contact from his first trip to Russia. The man was ecstatic to hear they had brought one hundred Russian Bibles, but he was skittish, too. He had been tortured many times by the Russian secret police. Caught in the smuggling of one hundred Bibles, which the Russian Communists labeled pornography, would get a man sent to the dreaded Siberian labor camps, or gulags, for a very long time!

"I'll have a man named Markov get in touch with you," the contact whispered and then scurried off.

Markov was so bold he took Andrew's breath away. "We'll make the exchange near Red Square," he said. "No one would expect such a crazy thing."

"Get smart—lose your mind," muttered Andrew.

Unbelievably, Andrew found himself parking the Opel near the great red-brick wall around the Kremlin. Markov drove up in his small car and parked. Andrew asked Hans to pray while the other two hurriedly transferred the Bibles into Markov's car. Markov could barely suppress a grin. Andrew was petrified.

"Goodbye, friend," chirped Markov. "Soon churches all over Russia will have Bibles!"

Andrew didn't begin to relax until they had left the campground and the vicinity of Moscow. He drove south into the Ukraine. It was in the Ukraine near Kiev that he saw a miracle. His contact there showed him a tiny Ukrainian Bible. It was so small it would fit in a shirt pocket.

"But it must be only a few books of the Bible," insisted Andrew, who knew something about Bibles.

"No, it is complete," said the contact, enjoying Andrew's amazement.

Andrew examined the pages of the tiny Ukrainian

Bible in awe. The paper was the thinnest he had ever seen. Yet the tiny type was crisp and completely legible. To a smuggler it was like finding a diamond. Imagine how many more Bibles—in any language—he could bring to these Communist countries if they were as tiny as this one! He must have it. He must be able to show it to the Bible societies in Holland. It was proof that it could be done. It was the only time Andrew ever traded Bibles.

His contact didn't mind at all. "Why should I mind getting two Bibles for one!"

But Andrew did not get the tiny Bible back to Holland. As they were leaving the Ukraine he encountered a pastor who ministered to a congregation of one thousand but did not have a single Bible. Andy had no choice. He gave the pastor his tiny Bible. The Bible societies in Holland would just have to take his word that such a tiny Bible could be printed.

Back in Holland his mission work entered a new phase. He was obsessed with the idea of miniature Bibles. He met with his suppliers. Many of the Bibles to the Communist countries had been supplied free by the British and foreign Bible societies. The Russian and Ukrainian Bibles had been supplied free by the American Bible Society. But the Bible societies had limited resources.

"We can't print such an exquisitely tiny Bible in small quantities," they reluctantly told Andrew.

But Andrew could not let the idea die. He began to consider printing such a Bible himself. Meanwhile he and Hans recruited a third member of the team, a bold young seminarian named Rolf. Rolf was reluctant, though. Had he gone to seminary to do this? For the first time Andrew's vehicle, loaded with Bibles, set off without him. Hans and a grumbling Rolf took Bibles to one of the most difficult Communist countries, Romania. In spite of all the obstacles there, they distributed their Bibles. Rolf came back beaming and enthusiastic for his new mission for Christ. "How the Romanians hunger for the Bible," he admitted.

Andrew had submitted bids to various printers for the tiny Bibles he wanted. An English printer could produce them for three dollars apiece, but only for a print run of five thousand copies. That meant fifteen thousand dollars was needed. Andrew and Corrie agreed they could sell their house, if necessary, to raise the money. Even Andrew wondered if this weren't beyond the call of their duty, especially when Corrie gave birth to their fourth child, a girl they christened Stephanie. Providentially, they didn't have to sell the house. The Dutch Bible Society agreed to fund the entire cost if Andrew reimbursed them half the cost as he used the Bibles. This he felt he could manage. Money was becoming less of a problem as the word spread around western Europe of his amazing success behind the Iron Curtain.

By 1964, Andrew's small operation had purchased a van. That summer while Hans took the Opel to Hungary, Andrew and Rolf loaded the van with 650 tiny Russian Bibles and drove to Moscow. Though recently married, Rolf was not about to abandon his mission. His new bride pitched in to help Corrie run Andrew's operation in Holland. Once again, Andrew made contact with Markov through the one Protestant church in Moscow. This time, though, they transferred their cargo in a less conspicuous place than Red Square. "A shopping area where dozens of people are loading boxes into cars and trucks certainly seems wiser," commented a thankful Rolf.

For nearly ten years Andrew's organization, which always seemed a small seat-of-the-pants operation, had systematically introduced small numbers of Bibles to Communist countries behind the Iron Curtain. Only the completely closed, rabidly Communist country of Albania had escaped his smuggling. His organization of five kept the two vehicles as busy as five humans could. Andrew now went on speaking tours as the mysterious Brother Andrew, and in 1965 came to the United States. He had always resisted going to America because so many Europeans went there—it seemed to him, with their tails between their legs—begging for money. He would not do that.

But on the other hand, would he forever exclude the United States from hearing about his work? That didn't seem fair either. Once in Holland a sincere American had approached him after a talk with that very question. "Brother Andrew," gushed the American, "you must come to the United States. The people there must also know what is going on in Communist countries."

Later Andrew was contacted by the American, who claimed to be a theological student. Funds were available from his school for Andrew to come on a speaking tour. Andrew accepted, but when he arrived there he knew something was very wrong. The students carried rifles.

"But what is this?" he asked his host in amazement.

"How can you ask? You know what the Communists are like. We are preparing for an invasion from the south. Mexico is full of Communists. We will fight them to the last man."

Andrew shrugged off the wild remark as the overheated

imagination of a young man. He knew that hyperactive, hostile type of person very well. He had once been that same way as a soldier. That night Andrew spoke to the school about what he now called the "Suffering Church" in Europe and Asia. After the talk his host stormed up to him.

"What was that sob story all about? You were supposed to blast the Commies. You were supposed to encourage us to fight the red menace to the death."

Andrew knew now he had made a huge mistake going there. "That isn't my mission," he explained patiently. "I tell people in the West what is happening to their Christian brothers and sisters behind the Iron Curtain. I don't publicly attack the Communist systems. It's hard enough for me to get in and out of those countries."

"Then what use are you to us? To our cause? You've embarrassed me enough, Brother Andrew. I am afraid we can no longer fund your trip."

That night Andrew, who was almost destitute, left what must have been some kind of military school and moved into a rundown motel. He wired Corrie in Holland for money. Meanwhile, as he waited, he lived on milk and yogurt he bought from a nearby convenience store. Finally, the money arrived. Then, just as he made arrangements to leave, he received an invitation to speak at a theological seminary. Why not? It would help justify his trip. But he was stunned when only three people showed up for his talk. How many bad judgments about America could he make? He remembered his nightmare trip to Bulgaria and calmed down. Maybe something good would come out of it. Following God wasn't always a path through a rose garden.

141

On the West Coast, where he was going to fly out, he was invited to speak at a large church. He threw his heart and soul into a sermon on the Suffering Church. Some in the congregation were openly weeping. The pastor nodded his approval as Andrew sat down—and then he made an impassioned plea for new seat cushions!

I hate to admit it, God, Andrew silently fumed, but Americans are just as I imagined them—selfish.

He couldn't wait to leave. But before he left Los Angeles he was introduced to a man named John Sherrill who had been giving speeches, too, but about his miraculous recovery from cancer. Sherrill, a writer who had worked for *Reader's Digest,* was then with *Guideposts* magazine in New York. He spoke politely to Andrew about his cancer, but he had a reporter's nose. As he pried facts from Andrew, he grew more and more excited. He invited Andrew to have breakfast with him at his hotel the next morning. There he made no pretense about not being aware of a great story. Andrew talked nonstop for three hours.

"We've got to get your story out," cried Sherrill. "I'll get it into *Guideposts* as soon as possible."

Praise God for some enthusiasm from at least one American, Andrew told himself. Perhaps the *Guideposts* article, if Sherrill actually ever got around to writing it, might interest some people. Then Andrew impulsively flew west from Los Angeles. Maybe he could still justify his disappointing trip to America.

He flew across the Pacific Ocean to Hong Kong. From there he intended to enter the Communist country of China. "Red China," the most heavily populated country in the world, hid behind what westerners called the "Bamboo

Curtain." One of the hard-line Communist countries like Russia or Romania, China might even be as bad as Albania. Andrew intended to find out. In Moscow he had met many Chinese who suggested he try to come there. Surely, Andrew reasoned, many Christians must remain in China, left over from a century of intense mission work. He couldn't have gone to school at the WEC, an organization founded by the famous Chinese missionary C. T. Studd, without knowing a lot about China.

But in Hong Kong people told Andrew, "What planet have you been living on? You can't get into China. No one can."

Brother Andrew was told that even the famous missionary Gladys Aylward, who had become a Chinese citizen, had given up trying to get back into Red China. She was on the island of Taiwan, a little democratic China started by the deposed leader Chiang Kai-shek. There she contented herself by running an orphanage. But Andrew saw his total unfamiliarity with China as an advantage. The Chinese Communists didn't know him either. As stubborn as ever, he went to the travel office maintained by the Red Chinese in Hong Kong and applied for a visa. They took his passport with his application, and told him he would have an answer in three days.

Later that day a missionary who had once served in China scoffed, "My friend, 'three days' is Chinese for 'never'!"

But God had done the 'impossible' for Andrew before. Andrew had not stopped praying since he landed in Hong Kong. On the third day he went to the travel office where a poker-faced official handed him his passport—and a visa! Then Andrew did what he had always done. He bought Bibles, but these were in Mandarin, the dialect of Chinese chosen by the Communists as the official language of China. When he entered China, a customs official looked inside his bag directly at the Bibles. Andrew waited for the ax to fall.

"Do you have a camera?" asked the official.

Andrew said no and proceeded into China. He could only conclude that Bibles were virtually unknown to most Chinese. Then he found out the truth: He could not give his Bibles away! In the seventeen years since the Communists took over China by force, they had virtually destroyed every vestige of Christianity. They had run out all the missionaries and executed thousands of Chinese Christians. Now Christianity was permitted, but no one seemed interested. Religion in any form was scorned.

"Religion is for weaklings," snorted one man. "China is no longer weak!"

Slowly Andrew learned just what the Chinese Communists had done to the church. The Communist government in the 1950s decided to strangle what remained of the old mainline denominations in China by establishing a state-sanctioned church. The "Three-Self Patriotic Movement" church became the only legal church in Red China. "Self-governing, self-supporting, self-propagating" was its phony slogan. For the good of the Communist state, the church had certain regulations and restrictions. Every pastor and every member had to be registered. This alone was enough to scare away many believers. But the pastor was also forbidden to evangelize or teach religion to children. This almost guaranteed the church could not grow. In addition, he could not preach on tithing, Sunday as a day of rest, healing, or the Second Coming of Christ. The sermons became sterile, boring recitations on morality. The government strategy worked.

"The 'Three-Self' churches are little attended and the mainline denominations have vanished," concluded Andrew.

When Andrew returned to Holland he realized more than ever he needed more workers in his organization. He wanted to visit every European Communist country at least once a year. And he wanted to blaze new ground. The Gospel must be brought once again to Red China. One defeat meant nothing. The early Christians were repulsed again and again by Rome. But after 300 years, suddenly the Roman emperor Constantine vaulted Christianity into the forefront.

Still, Andrew was very suspicious of volunteers. His work was so demanding. And he had many contacts behind the Iron Curtain whose lives were in jeopardy. Would a volunteer crumble under the pressure of interrogation? Would a volunteer betray his contacts? Many times in the past Andrew had told would-be volunteers that once they had penetrated Communist countries themselves, they could look him up. No one ever came back to look him up. No one, that is, until Marcus.

Marcus was a young Dutchman Andrew had talked to at a Bible school in Wales. One day he showed up in Sint Pancras. "I went into Yugoslavia as you suggested and I passed out tracts. Now here I am, reporting for work."

"I promised you, that is true," said an amazed Andrew. "Now you can go with Rolf into Yugoslavia and Bulgaria."

And off the two young Dutchmen went.

eleven

Shortly after Rolf took Marcus into eastern Europe, Andrew and Hans flew to Cuba. In 1965 Cuban officials hated Americans, not Dutchmen, and Andrew received little trouble from the police. He was allowed to speak in churches, but only because of the weakened state of the church. The Cuban Communists had attacked the church through its clergy. Clergy were classified by the Communist government as nonproductive slugs, and as such, they were issued no food or clothing coupons. They were often thrown into work gangs with criminals, homosexuals, and drug addicts. Many clergy were sweating in the sugar cane fields.

"Authorities are sure both the clergy and the churches will eventually die," Andrew observed.

But he also observed that Cubans were thirsty for God. Their Communist dictator Fidel Castro had only been in power since 1959, and apparently, they still received much

news from abroad. Many asked Andrew about Billy
Graham. They asked in disbelief about the "God is dead"
movement. Cuba did not lack Bibles. That was good
because it was very difficult to bring material into Cuba by
plane. But Andrew knew the Christians in Cuba needed
encouragement. The church must be strengthened.

Stopping over in the United States, Andrew learned
from John Sherrill that he had indeed written an article
about him for *Guideposts*. According to Sherrill, the
response had been tremendous. Americans were astonished
that anyone was courageous enough to smuggle Bibles
behind the Iron Curtain. Sherrill and his wife Elizabeth
wanted very much to do a full book on Andrew. Judging
from the response to the magazine article, the book had a
chance to be a best-seller. Then Sherrill told him that perhaps many thousands would read about the Suffering
Church. Andrew should consider what that might mean for
his ministry. Andrew suppressed the pride he felt as the
object of a best-selling book. He had to think straight. If the
book were really popular, he might not ever be able to enter
the Iron Curtain countries again! He had to weigh the pros
and cons. He prayed. He recalled his sudden impulse to go
to Red China. Wasn't that right after he met John Sherrill?
Had God been nudging Andrew in new directions?

"I'll do it. If God allows the book to be a best-seller,
then it means He wants me to concentrate on other countries. Hopefully my colleagues will still be able to travel
behind the Iron Curtain."

The Sherrill writing team interviewed Andrew exten-
sively. They promised to keep his real name secret. In fact,
they would change many names. Even Sint Pancras would

get another name. Meanwhile Andrew and his group continued their work.

The year 1966 brought their first incursion into Albania. Amazingly, Rolf and Marcus were in the first tour group allowed into the country. Albania was unusual in almost every respect. There was no Albanian Bible in any one of their native tongues, and there never had been. Christians used a Bible that was either in Latin or in Greek. Nevertheless, the two Dutchmen carried Christian tracts in three of the native languages. But Rolf and Marcus quickly discovered that Albania was the most extreme police state of all the Communist countries. The people were suspicious to the point of refusing to speak. Offering them a tract was futile. They would clasp their hands behind their backs. They would squeeze their eyes shut. In desperation, the two Dutchmen left a pile of tracts on a bench along a busy street. The police stopped the tour group later and demanded to know who had left the tracts on the bench. Rather than cause the entire tour group to be expelled from Albania, Marcus and Rolf confessed. The police warned them, then returned the tracts. Not one tract had been taken!

"Albania is the grimmest place yet," admitted Andrew when Rolf and Marcus returned.

Nevertheless, they would continue to probe Albania, as well as the second hardest place to evangelize: Red China. Andrew's group had now grown to eleven: six men and five women. For a while he wanted it no larger. He told them he wanted an organism, not an organization. If other groups were inspired to do the same thing, so much the better. But he would not recruit any more workers. The only concession he made was occasionally to take someone outside his group on one of the smuggling trips. But that adventure was not followed by an offer of a position in his organism.

The Communist countries were not monolithic. Some remained rigid, whereas some seemed slowly to relax their Marxist isolation. By 1967 it was legal to take Bibles into Yugoslavia. Even Russia was changing. The western countries were shocked when Russia Communists allowed the publication of Aleksandr Solzhenitsyn's grim novel about modern Russia, *One Day in the Life of Ivan Denisovich.* It may have been part of campaign to discredit the original Russian Communist dictator Joseph Stalin but it nevertheless signaled a major easing of censorship in Russia.

"We pray," said friends of Andrew, "that ever so slowly the European Communists really are allowing more freedoms."

On the other hand, China had suffered a major setback in 1966. The western countries watched in horror as the dictator Mao Tse-tung unloosed young hooligans called the Red Guards in what he dubbed a "Cultural Revolution." These guards took particular delight in humiliating the educated and privileged. To many westerners it seemed like watching the French Revolution in the 1790s when the peasants went berserk against the aristocracy. But the Cultural Revolution had a dire effect on religion. Vestiges of Christianity, which had been largely ignored, were actively persecuted by the rampaging Red Guards. Christianity was not as dead as Andrew had concluded from his first trip to Red China. He had since learned of three there who continued to lead the fight for Christ: Watchman Nee,

Wang Ming-Tao, and Mama Kwang. Scorning the phony Three-Self churches, they had set up tiny congregations called "house churches." But all three leaders were now in prison. How Andrew wanted to get help now to the Suffering Church in Red China!

"But our funds are so limited," groaned Andrew.

That would soon change. In 1967 Andrew's work was revealed to the general public in *God's Smuggler,* published by New American Library. The title bothered Andrew since it hinted at criminal activity. But the book by the Sherrill team sold well, and then caught fire. Several large American newspapers gave it good reviews. Religious notables like Norman Vincent Peale and Catherine Marshall recommended it. To Andrew's surprise, the book brought a blessing he hadn't even considered: Money earned by his share of the royalties from the book gushed in. Now he could buy needed office equipment. He could pay for the printing of Bibles. He could buy vehicles. "We can even get real mechanics to maintain them," chorused his grateful team members.

Money from the book spawned some wild scheming as well. If it became more difficult to penetrate the Iron Curtain countries in vehicles because of their fame, how else might they get the Bibles in? Imaginatively, they pictured loads of Bibles carried in by helium balloons. They considered ultralight aircraft that could skim below radar detection and drop bundles of Bibles. They liked the idea of a midget submarine landing near an unguarded beach. But not all their scheming was about the Iron Curtain countries. Andrew had decided many months before that perhaps God wanted him to evangelize elsewhere. And

151

perhaps not Red China or Cuba. Perhaps not even a Communist country at all!

"Brother Andrew, would you be interested in visiting Saudi Arabia?" an Englishman had asked him in 1967.

When Andrew learned this English scholar was going to do nothing less than try to find the real Mount Sinai, he knew this was an opportunity of a lifetime. If a door opened, he walked through it. He believed completely that the Lord's words in Revelation 3:8 were meant for him: "I know thy works: behold, I have set before thee an open door, and no man can shut it: for thou hast a little strength, and hast kept my word, and hast not denied my name." Perhaps this scholar might be looking for Mount Sinai, but Andrew would be walking through an open door intent on exploring the minds and hearts of the Arabs. Arabs were Muslims, of course, and their public posture emphasized rabid opposition to other beliefs.

"But they are, nevertheless, spiritual cousins of Jews and Christians," reasoned Andrew optimistically.

The ultimate authority for Muslims is the Koran, a book of God's words delivered by angelic messengers to the prophet Mohammed several centuries after Christ was crucified. The Koran nowhere directly quotes the Old or New Testaments, but it does acknowledge Abraham, Moses, David, and Jesus as holy prophets who preceded Mohammed. According to Muslims, Mohammed was the Seal of the Prophets; he was to be the last. It was Mohammed who on Judgment Day would intercede for mankind with God, or Allah. Mohammed considered himself a continuation of Jewish-Christian revelation and was angry when both groups rejected his teachings. From what Andrew had heard,

Muslims were still angry about his rejection.

"The Allah-worshipping Muslim world is quite a different task from the godless Communist world," reflected Andrew.

At the Beirut Baptist Seminary in Lebanon Andrew rendezvoused with his English host and Doug, a man from the Youth With a Mission organization. There the Englishman purchased a used but rugged Land Rover. To the equipment they loaded in the Land Rover, Andrew added boxes of Bibles in Arabic! The adventurers drove east to Damascus in Syria, then south into Jordan. The rough road aggravated Andrew's chronically sore back. Then on the outskirts of Amman the Englishman rear-ended a car on a blind curve! The Jordanian driver was furious. A loud argument broke out as they awaited the police. Andrew whispered to his friends the name of his contact in Amman and quietly slipped away.

That evening Andrew met his contact and preached in a church in Amman. For another two days he enjoyed the fellowship of Christians at the fringe of the Muslim world. It was only then that his two traveling companions showed up. They had been in jail all that time! They were now anxious to depart Amman in the dented Land Rover. But they were not discouraged. All they could talk about was Mount Sinai. Many scholars questioned the traditional location of Mount Sinai on the Sinai Peninsula. After all, when Moses first fled Egypt as a young man, he went to Midian, which was in modern-day Saudi Arabia. What would be more natural for him as an older man during the Exodus than to seek refuge in Midian? And there he ascended Mount Sinai. "So the real Mount Sinai is in Saudi

Arabia," speculated the English scholar.

As they approached the Saudi Arabian border, Andrew was as excited as he had been for a long time. Like Moses he felt a "stranger in a strange land"! Near the Gulf of Aqaba they reached the border crossing into Saudi Arabia. Once again Andrew prayed while guards were blind to his Bibles. But something went wrong. The Saudis would not let the Englishman or his Land Rover in! The Englishman urged Andrew and the other man to continue on the mission if they could. In disbelief Andrew and Doug collected their things. Andrew packed as many of the Bibles as he could carry, and then they hired a taxi to drive them south into Saudi Arabia. As they skirted Medina, one of Mohammed's holy places, they noticed a sign that read INFIDELS FORBIDDEN. Near another holy site, Mecca, they stopped in Jidda. There Andrew had the name of a contact. His contact was amazed. He had never met another Christian in the area.

His contact was frightened, too. "Not only are churches banned, but any overt show of Christianity is strictly forbidden."

Andrew and Doug horrified the contact by going to the local bazaar to hand out Bibles in Arabic! It was such an outrageous act that no one quite understood what they were doing. It was virtually suicide to do such a thing. But having done it, Andrew and Doug calmly obtained exit visas and departed Saudi Arabia from the Jidda airport. The trip had been flawed nearly every step of the way but Andrew was pleased. He had penetrated Saudi Arabia and, in so doing, had a real taste of the Muslim world. Now he knew just how difficult it would be to carry the Gospel into such a world. And who knew how many lives were changed by the Bibles he and Doug distributed in Jidda? Andrew never underestimated the power of the Bible.

Andrew was heartened later to find that his English friend had safely returned to Europe. Of course, by that time Andrew was probing other directions. Often now he thought about Africa, China, and Latin America. He even went to Vietnam for a while. The country was in a civil war between Communists and non-Communists. The United States had sent troops in to help the non-Communists. Andrew wanted to assess their need for Bibles, but his inquiries brought into focus his other recent desire, smuggling Bibles into Red China. Someone told him about an American ex-Marine working for a Christian radio station in the Philippine city of Manila. This ex-Marine was contacting people on the Chinese mainland. He was actually recruiting Chinese to store Bibles after they were smuggled in! Andrew was amazed. It was so seldom he encountered other people who did what he did.

"But on the negative side," reflected Andrew, "the ex-Marine might ruin all future projects if his efforts are discovered by the Communist authorities in Red China."

Although Andrew wrote the ex-Marine a letter, like other missionaries in Vietnam, he was soon overwhelmed by the war. When they weren't treating the sick and wounded, they were taking in orphans. While there, Andrew discovered a vile practice: Vietnamese sold children into slavery. He decided then and there he must help ransom these children. But the war was expanding tremendously. Half a million American troops and many thousands of their allies were fighting Communist guerillas all over Vietnam. Although

Andrew had little fear of combat, he was not as foolhardy as he had once been as a soldier. "Dying in the crossfire of a civil war will scarcely advance the Gospel," he admitted.

Nevertheless, he recruited in Holland for his fledgling operation in Vietnam, and young Johan Companjen answered the call. Andrew knew Johan must be deeply committed. He had left behind his fiancée Anneke and a bright career in engineering to answer the call of missions. Besides that, the attitude in Holland was that the war was a crazy American enterprise. Andrew had counseled Johan in the past, hinting the youth was still putting conditions on his will to serve God. "I'll serve You, God, but please, not in Vietnam!" simply wouldn't do.

It was the venerable Corrie ten Boom who may have convinced Johan. "Oh, don't worry if the world says you are insane to go to Vietnam because it is so dangerous," she counseled Johan. "The safest place on earth is in the center of God's will. You must decide if God wants you in Vietnam." Because Johan felt sure God wanted him in Vietnam, he left to serve a one-year apprenticeship at the orphanage, before returning to Holland to marry Anneke.

One great friendship Andrew cemented while in Vietnam was with his countrywoman Corrie ten Boom. At the time Corrie was a fiery evangelist of seventy-five from Haarlem. She was well known for her family's efforts to harbor Jews and other refugees from the Nazis during World War II. She had suffered greatly in a German work camp, not the least horror of which was watching her beloved sister die. When the war was over she was a worn-out, beat-up, fifty-three-year-old, but she sought no rocking chair. Instead, she evangelized all over the world. A classic itinerant preacher, Corrie owned just two dresses. Many a soldier in Vietnam was startled to see a frumpy old lady crawl out of a Jeep.

"Let's talk turkey, boys!" she would snap. "If anything happens to you, are you ready to meet the Lord?"

Corrie was a firecracker. And she was just about the best storyteller Andrew had ever heard. Besides Vietnam and the countries of Europe, she had been to Cuba, South Africa, Japan, Bermuda, New Zealand, Australia, Taiwan, Israel, India, Argentina, Korea, Uganda, Rwanda, and dozens of others. Over sixty in all, she said. Andrew wanted to know all about the countries he had never visited. It was possibly Corrie ten Boom, more than anyone, who spurred his interest in Africa. Many Christian workers had labored there. There were tens of millions of black Christians in Africa. But their need was still very great. Many African countries were now experimenting with Communism, relentlessly pushed by Russia and Red China with offers of money and technical help. Among the first countries to succumb to this temptation were Angola, Mozambique, and Uganda. With the introduction of Communism came the losses of freedoms that always follow. Missionaries were rounded up and expelled or imprisoned. Churches were shut down or tightly controlled. Publishing of Bibles ceased.

"Shortage of Bibles?" observed Andrew, his pulse suddenly racing. It was time to see for himself. Soon Andrew and his group were making trips to Africa.

By this time Andrew was calling his organization "Open Doors," a name inspired by Revelation 3:8. Besides the original office in Holland, Open Doors maintained offices in the United States, England, and Asia. Now he wanted an Open Doors office in Africa but he did not want to place it in the troubled areas of central Africa. Andrew had in mind the very stable country of South Africa. Although he abhorred South Africa's policy of apartheid, which not only kept the races apart but one race prosperous and the other race destitute, he had to have a stable platform to begin his work. He set an example by insisting that all meetings must be integrated. But given the conditions of the country, he found many meetings all black or all white. He was amazed at how blind the whites were to injustice in their country. Whites would listen to his stories of smuggling Bibles, exuding admiration for what he had done.

"How can we help you smuggle Bibles into Russia?" they clamored.

Then he would spring his trap. "Do you employ black servants?" he would casually ask his white audience.

"Well, sure," they admitted and shrugged. Didn't everyone?

"Did you give them Bibles? Did you share your faith with them?"

"What!" they would gasp.

Andrew tried to control his temper. "I certainly don't want your help with Bibles to Russia if you're neglecting your own brothers and sisters right here in South Africa!"

Andrew also warned them that they could no longer hide their heads in the sand. Africa was changing. They had better take care of their apartheid problem before it was too late. They must do away with that evil system and accept black Africans as their brothers and sisters. As

Andrew traveled around Africa from his base, he evolved a plan for Africa. But he saw the 1970s not as a time to switch all his efforts to Africa, but as a time to attack on several fronts, simultaneously if possible!

Was the older Andrew so different from the younger one who once cried, "Get smart—lose your mind"?

His China dream would not go away. In 1970 the ex-Marine in Manila, whom Andrew called Brother David, came to Holland. David was a powerfully built man, but he impressed Andrew more with his reliance on the Bible for guidance. David prefaced his dream with Mark 13:10: "And the gospel must first be published among all nations." "Published?" questioned Andrew in surprise. Then he learned David was even more qualified for the China project than he had realized. David was also a competent printer! Soon the two like minds raced ahead with great possibilities. Why not print a small red New Testament the exact size of the "Little Red Book" of the Communist dictator Mao's sayings that was handed out all over Red China?

"Why not print ten million?" suggested David.

Andrew gulped. "Perhaps not quite that many to start with," he counseled. But Andrew did approve the printing of twenty-five thousand. Meanwhile David was also to contact everyone necessary for such a venture. To have support in this massive effort, David was officially added to the staff of Open Doors in Asia.

Andrew continued to push efforts by Open Doors, which he often called his ministry to the Suffering Church, in Europe, Latin America, Africa, and Asia. But a trip to the United States in 1971 set Andrew back. Andrew had set up a small office in Salida, Colorado. One day his friend Don was going to fly him to a meeting in Denver. The Beechcraft Debonair climbed off the runway to a height of about five hundred feet. Suddenly, the engine went dead.

Andrew's stomach vaulted into his mouth. "Say! What's going on?" he cried.

"We're crashing," replied Don dryly.

The noise became deafening as pain jolted Andrew's back. Dust billowed around the windows. He looked over at Don. Don's face was covered with blood. Don was clawing at his seatbelt.

"Get out!" screamed Don. "We just fueled up!"

Andrew unbuckled his belt and hammered the door open with the butt of his hand. Almost paralyzed with pain, he fell out of the plane. After a few yards of crawling, pain completely immobilized him. He must have been on an anthill because black ants scurried frantically before his eyes.

"Praise God, we're alive," he said, not caring if a hundred ants bit him or not.

Moments later he heard a siren. Pain shot though every nerve as paramedics stabilized him on a stretcher. He was lifted into an ambulance. He must have been given him a painkiller because soon he felt nothing at all. At the hospital he was told Don's injuries were superficial. That was the good news. The bad news was that Andrew had a broken back but there probably was no damage to the spinal cord. With that knowledge, Andrew called Corrie in Holland. His wife's voice triggered all the anxiety he had built up over several hours. He broke down.

"I'll come there as soon as possible," she promised.

The more he found out about the accident, the more blessed he felt. The plane could have easily plunged down into a deep, deadly ravine. He heard one of the rescue crew was a pastor, who quickly started a prayer chain that included several churches and two Christian conferences. Andrew was absolutely sure those prayers had helped Don and him. And it would help their healing, too.

In the meantime, Andrew could only wait for Corrie.

twelve

When Corrie arrived in Colorado she found Andrew encased in a plaster cast from his armpits to his hips. In one way his immobility proved a boon. Corrie and Andrew could spend time together, with many hours devoted to Bible study.

"Never did I realize before," said Andrew, "how my busy life robbed me of the deep pleasures of Scripture."

He enjoyed those pleasures for several months, too, as it was that long before doctors removed his plaster cast. His back had healed so well the x-rays could barely detect fractures in his vertebrae. "Oh, the power of prayer!" insisted Andrew gleefully.

Just as incredible was that his chronic back pain was gone. For eighteen years he had not dared dig in a garden or ride a bicycle. Now back in Holland, at age forty-three, Andrew even took up running again. He was soon actively continuing his Open Doors activities in Europe and Latin

America, while he refined the mission's operations in Africa and Asia.

By 1975 Andrew decided he must go more public with his efforts for China. He and Brother David contacted religious groups all over the world. Would they participate in a "Love China" conference in the Philippines? Judiciously, Andrew set conditions for the conference. The conferees must express their love for the Chinese people. There must be no anti-Communist rhetoric. The conference was wholly about bringing Jesus to Red China. In September 1975 hundreds of delegates from fifty-five different mission organizations and twenty-three countries convened for five days in Manila. Andrew was gratified that major news organization decided to cover the conference.

The conference was a complete education on China. Some speakers detailed the history of the church in China. Some explained the state of the church there under Mao. Some clarified the differences among the teachings of Marx, Lenin, Mao, and Christ. Several speakers told how Chinese Christians suffered today for the sake of Jesus. And, as Andrew always insisted, God's help had to be petitioned by prayer, much prayer. The lives of almost one billion Chinese were at stake.

Andrew may have discouraged anti-Communist rhetoric but he did set a tough tone.

"Organizations and missions that explicitly state that they only work in countries where this is legal are missing the boat. . .We have to live a life that is more revolutionary than that of the revolutionaries."[1]

Samuel Moffatt, a missionary from Korea, shared Andrew's tough talk.

"The Chinese Communists have outdisciplined us, outworked us, and outcommitted us. Unless we are willing to match their commitment in our service for the Lord, we are never going to make a difference there."[2]

But Andrew grew more and more frustrated. Comments from many delegates made it clear they were far too timid to join the fight. "The door to China is closed," they admitted almost in defeat. "When God is ready, He will let us in." Andrew couldn't believe his ears. Those were the same weak objections the Englishman William Carey had heard back in the 1700s!

In any event, the landscape of China changed radically within just one year after the conference. First Chou En-lai and then Mao Tse-tung himself died. The two most powerful leaders in China were dead! Their successors, while not honorable by western standards, proved a vast improvement in leadership. Christians began to smuggle Bibles into China on a small scale. Andrew was getting very excited about David's plan to introduce thousands of Bibles in one colossal caper. "We must make Brother David's plan work," reflected Andrew. "The moment to evangelize China is ripe."

Meanwhile by the mid-1970s, from his Open Doors base in South Africa, Andrew and his colleagues visited Zambia, Rhodesia, Malawi, and other African countries. Africans were open to the Gospel. In Rwanda, a country that had suffered every disaster known to man, Andrew told eager listeners about a pastor imprisoned in Russia. He found that when black Africans learned whites also suffered at the hands of whites, they began to accept whites as something more than just oppressors. But Andrew found his heart breaking when young Rwandans took up a collection for the Russian pastor. These poor Rwandans did not have enough money to feed themselves properly. Africans also found a great bond with the suffering Christ.

"Yes," lamented Andrew, "they understand persecution and suffering only too well."

Andrew visited dozens of African countries, and in each one he established contacts. As a matter of course, he spoke to some people with blood on their hands. But he could not refuse to see anyone. Over several years he met the Christian leaders in each country and learned their churches' greatest needs. Soon he planned a "Love Africa" conference patterned after the modestly successful Love China conference. By 1978 Love Africa was a reality. In Malawi, a tiny country along the side of Lake Nyassa, 250 delegates from thirty-seven African countries met. All the delegations represented countries south of the Sahara Desert. The northern African countries Andrew considered part of his yet unrealized "Muslim effort."

Love Africa was a limited success as racial tensions still soured many discussions. But Andrew was sure it was a beginning. He tried to convince the conferees that blacks and whites must unite to fight the persecution of Christians. Once again, Andrew saw the irony of how their attention was riveted by persecution outside of Africa. This they could look at with profound sympathy. An evangelist from Russia held them spellbound, even though Andrew had to translate his broken German into English, which in turn had to be translated by another into French!

After Love Africa, Open Doors teams continued to visit African countries. A favorite expression of Andrew's was, "You cannot spell the word Gospel or even God without first spelling 'go.' "[3] In Mozambique, for example, Open Doors established a school to train hundreds of pastors. For once the emphasis was not on Bibles. Since many black ministers never attended Bible college or seminary, Andrew felt it was essential to teach them solid scriptural truths. Their instructors were fellow African ministers. This work was called Project Timothy, after the young disciple trained by the Apostle Paul. Each student was provided a "Victory Manual" that told how to stand firm during persecution. The final two sentences read:

"Why are some able to stand? Because they
have learned how to sink their roots of faith
deeply into the rock, Jesus Christ."[4]

Andrew also went to Uganda, where Corrie ten Boom had evangelized. Winston Churchill had once called the former British colony the "Pearl of Africa." But since 1971, the country had been under the rule of the dictator Idi Amin. The outlook for Christians was not good, even though sixty percent of Ugandans were Christian. Amin was a huge, affable man, skilled at making a good impression. But behind the grinning moon face was the mind of a ruthless killer. Idi Amin was a Muslim of the Kakwa tribe.

In 1976 Andrew met the Anglican archbishop Janani

Luwum. Janani was head chaplain of the Ugandan army. "Brother Andrew," he confided, "most of our soldiers are Christian, but we have no Bibles for them."

Andrew did not hesitate. "How many do you need?"

"Fifty thousand."

Andrew had long given up his reservations about raising money in the United States. God had bestowed great wealth on that country. And many Americans wanted to help Open Doors. It was not long before Janani Luwum had the fifty thousand Bibles.

If Idi Amin had not been so murderous, his regime would have been comical. His death squads were men in dark glasses, flowered shirts, bell-bottom trousers, and elevator shoes. They murdered his enemies, often in broad daylight. Shortly after Andrew met Archbishop Luwum, the archbishop presented Idi Amin with a petition against the killing signed by Ugandan religious leaders. Andrew was told the enraged Amin personally shot the archbishop through the mouth.

When Andrew learned of this atrocity he knew he must show support for the Christians in Uganda. The occasion he chose was the hundredth anniversary of the Anglican church in Uganda. In June 1977 Andrew flew into Kampala with two coworkers. The Entebbe airport there was itself quite a story. Just the previous year Palestinian terrorists had hijacked an Israeli airliner with one hundred passengers and forced it to land there. They were sure a fellow killer like Amin would welcome them, and they were right. What they did not reckon on was one of the most daring commando raids in history. Israelis rescued all the hostages. The airport was still littered with the planes the Israeli commandos destroyed.

One of Andrew's companions was Johan Companjen, who had served Open Doors in Vietnam. He had rejoined Open Doors in time to help with the Love China conference. Johan was a gifted speaker who often filled in for Andrew when he was too busy. Invariably by the time Johan, with his friendly broad Dutch face, was through speaking he had won the audience over. In his early thirties, Johan showed the greatest organizational skills of all Andrew's colleagues. Andrew would initiate contacts in countries with a broad agenda in mind, and Johan would be the facilitator. He took volumes of notes, systematized their efforts, and maintained personal contacts. Andrew was deeply impressed with Johan's maturity as a Christian, too.

As they prepared to leave the plane in Entebbe airport, Andrew said half-joking, "You know, Johan, it's not too late to change your mind."

In fact, Johan did not look well as he disembarked from the plane with Andrew. It was only later he admitted to Andrew that he was thinking very strongly about changing his mind. Even though Johan had survived terrible times in Vietnam, he did not face deadly situations with calm. His departure from the plane at Entebbe was to him one more momentous decision to face death for Christ.

In Kampala the Anglican church commemorated its anniversary in Namirembe Cathedral. Thousands gathered. But the air was electric with tension. What would the murderous Amin do to these celebrants? The congregation not only held the service but sang the "Martyrs' Hymn" as they slowly filed from the cathedral, then walked past Luwum's gravesite. Luwum's successor spoke over the grave of the "martyr who died for the nation."

That night Andrew and his two colleagues slept in the Kampala International Hotel. To their horror, Idi Amin's flower-shirted goon squads arrived that night. People were screaming in the halls as they were dragged out of their rooms. Yet the Dutchmen were not among the victims. The next day Andrew decided to try to get an audience with Amin. But an Anglican cleric changed his mind.

"You are on Idi Amin's death list," warned the cleric. "I know it for a fact. You must leave Uganda immediately."

When they called the airport to try to leave Uganda earlier than their booked flight, they were told it was impossible. The plane leaving that afternoon was already overbooked. The three prayed and proceeded to the Entebbe airport anyway. They were almost the first in line at the unmanned counter.

Finally a woman showed up at the counter. "We've lost our passenger list," she said, shaking her head. "So I'll just take you in order."

Once again the missionaries of Open Doors escaped death. Once again the lesson Andrew had learned at the WEC school in Scotland was confirmed. The missionary must trust God completely.

Andrew's many African trips did not keep him from his Asian projects. He had been wrong about the absence of Christianity on his visit in 1965. The church was not dead there. In fact, some westerners claimed the house church movement in China was the greatest movement of the Holy Spirit since Pentecost. Estimates of Chinese believers in the house churches ran up into the tens of millions. If that were true, it did seem truly a work of the Holy Spirit.

These house churches had no ordained ministers, denominations, or special buildings. And yet they thrived.

Andrew learned more about the miraculous efforts of Christians like Mama Kwang in southern China. She was the leading evangelist in China, and she and her husband had been imprisoned many times. Finally, their ministry had to go underground. In the cities her groups were often as small as three or four believers. These tiny bodies of believers were the house churches. But in rural areas, where the police were few and far between, as many as one thousand could congregate at a time, forming large house churches. But large or small, they all needed Bibles, so Mama Kwang appealed to Open Doors. This only confirmed what Brother Andrew insisted. Open Doors had to get Bibles into China on a large scale. "Just smuggling handfuls of Bibles in as tourists is not good enough," he stated.

Once Brother David, his wife, and four Chinese colleagues smuggled in nine hundred at one time. But Brother David knew more than anyone that an effort like that was not the answer. In 1979, after much prayer, the Kwangs left Red China. The move was controversial because many believers in China felt Mama Kwang was deserting them. Brother David rushed to Hong Kong to meet the Kwangs. They immediately began planning how to smuggle Bibles into China on a much larger scale than before.

"Our most immediate need is to get thirty thousand Bibles into the hands of local ministers," said Mama Kwang.

Every year in October the Canton Trade Fair welcomed groups of foreigners. They were given special treatment, including a mere wave through customs. Their luggage was not even inspected. Thus, with the help of Mama

Kwang, "Project Rainbow" was hatched. One group of thirty "businessmen," each carrying two large suitcases, would go into China for the trade fair. Each suitcase contained five hundred Bibles! These couriers would be able to deliver thirty thousand of the tiny New Testaments that Brother David had developed several years before.

"The greatest challenge to the couriers is the weight of the suitcases," explained Brother David. "Some of the couriers refer to this as 'Project Hernia'!"

Project Rainbow was a success, yet Brother David and his colleagues planned a project many times larger. Open Doors dubbed this new undertaking "Pearl" after the pearl of great price Jesus told of in Matthew 13. The Kwangs had the audacity to suggest one million Bibles could be delivered in one shipment! They knew of a fishing village on the south coast of China, about one hundred miles east of Hong Kong. Most of the villagers were Christians. If the Bibles could be delivered to a nearby beach, the villagers would take the Bibles from there. "But one million Bibles weigh 232 tons!" calculated someone.

Fortunately, Open Doors had a former naval officer code-named James among its contacts. James took over the logistics of delivering the cargo. He soon determined the only way to deliver such an enormous cargo was with a barge. "Bill," a former sea captain, was recruited. Bill saw no problem at all getting the Bibles near the beach in a barge pulled by a tugboat. To get the Bibles ashore he devised a scheme whereby watertight bundles of Bibles could be floated off the barge, then pulled to shore with small boats.

The enormity of the project became obvious when

Open Doors purchased a tug for $480,000! The generosity of America was never more apparent than when one congregation, Calvary Chapel in Costa Mesa, California, paid almost the entire cost of the tug. Open Doors called the tug *Michael* and its barge was *Gabriella*. Yes, the vessels were named after angels in the Bible, but these names were also used for Papa and Mama Kwang. The next step was getting the Bibles printed. Never had Open Doors done anything on such a large scale, and Thomas Nelson Publishers agreed to take on the task. "All costs of Project Pearl are projected to total about seven million dollars, or seven dollars per Bible," murmured Andrew in awe.

Andrew had to travel far and wide to raise the funds. At no cost to Open Doors, Pat Robertson of the Christian Broadcasting Network produced a promotional video for Andrew. It was ironic that Andrew publicly raised funds for such a dangerous, supposedly secret mission. Open Doors and the Kwangs also had many believers in China working on the project. Some located storage for such a huge volume of Bibles. Some enlisted helpers to unload the Bibles and transport them to the storehouses. Some monitored police activity. One Open Doors worker naïvely asked a group of five Chinese if they knew the risk they were taking. They patiently explained that the five of them had already spent a total of seventy-two years in prison!

Delivery was scheduled for the night before Easter Sunday on April 19, 1981. But Andrew had a nightmare that he felt might be a warning from God. After much prayer with other workers, Open Doors postponed the delivery. The Project Pearl team was devastated because they actually had the Bibles on the barge. Easter Sunday was spent by the crew of *Michael* in the Hong Kong harbor. Beside them bobbed one million Bibles aboard the *Gabriella*! The crew members wondered when the delivery would be made as the typhoon season was fast approaching. Finally, well into June, Andrew felt he had to let them proceed.

Mama Kwang sent word to the Chinese believers on the mainland:

> "By faith we are ready to move the patient if the hospital is ready to receive."[5]

The mainland Chinese were more than ready.

All around the world friends of Open Doors prayed for Project Pearl. As always, Andrew believed prayer was essential. At dusk on June 18 the tug *Michael* arrived at the destination. Captain Bill signaled the shore with a light. A light on shore signaled back. Three powerboats were lowered off the tug. One-ton bundles—232 in all—were put afloat. All the bundles were roped together so they could be pulled to shore in a massive chain. The powerboats towed the immensely heavy chain toward shore. Two thousand Chinese believers had descended onto the beach. They themselves formed a relay line that went out into the surf. As a bundle was beached it was cut open for its forty-eight boxes of Bibles. Then the line of people passed the boxes, each weighing about forty pounds, to safety above the beach. "There the Bibles will disappear into waiting cars, trucks, and bicycles," Brother David had said.

The actual transfer of the Bibles to the beach took only

two hours. Then the tug and barge left. Andrew learned only later that with one-third of the Bibles still on the beach the operation had been interrupted by an army patrol. But the patrol had not realized the scope of the operation. Who would have expected such a thing on an obscure little beach? The soldiers ineptly threw a few boxes into the sea, missing the huge cache still there. Even most of the Bibles they threw in the sea were later rescued and dried out. Only about ten thousand of the one million Bibles were permanently lost.

But some of the initial reports leaking out of China were pessimistic, perhaps intentionally. "Our western news organizations have immediately labeled the operation a poorly planned, silly failure," sighed Andrew.

To set the record straight, Open Doors decided to confide in a reporter from *Time* magazine. In October, *Time* reported Project Pearl as the success it was. But Andrew paid a heavy price for the coverage when *Time* blew his cover by giving his full name. Now his future travel anywhere would be severely compromised. Still, he knew he was in good company. The great missionary Gladys Aylward's identity had also once been betrayed by *Time*. That breech of faith almost resulted in her death at the hands of the Japanese in World War II. Her near-death put Andrew's own inconvenience in perspective.

Nonetheless, several missionary groups were very unhappy with the mixed publicity. Was Open Doors going to close China for all the other groups, too? Wasn't Open Doors flaunting its success? In retrospect, Andrew wished he had never granted *Time* the interview. Worse yet, the embarrassed Chinese authorities searched that much harder to find the smuggled Bibles. Some of Project Pearl's helpers in China were imprisoned and tortured.

One helper who was tortured was "Pastor John," who later said,

"I was surprised twice over the whole affair. First, that Christians, Chinese and Western, actually had the courage and the vision to mount something this big. And second, that it was never repeated."[6]

thirteen

I n the mid-1970s Andrew had to finally relent on his insistence to keep Open Doors a tiny organism. His ambitious Chinese and African projects required more offices and personnel. Still, with fewer than two hundred workers, Open Doors was small in comparison to other mission groups. Though few felt the religious pulse of foreign regimes like Andrew, he still occasionally had surprises. Once at a conference in the late 1970s a man stunned him.

"When are you going to come to our church in Iran?" he asked Andrew.

"Iran!" exclaimed Andrew.

At the time the despotic Muslim leader Ayatollah Khomeini held power in Iran. He hated the western democracies and Christians. With his approval Iranians held American embassy workers—supposedly safe from political chicanery—as hostages. Could there be a Christian church in Iran? Yet the man at the conference insisted that he was himself an evangelical pastor with a church in Iran.

"Yes," replied Andrew in amazement, "this we must see."

In the winter of 1981 Andrew and Johan flew into Tehran, the capital of Iran. The American hostages had been released, but the atmosphere, if not hostile, was chaotic. Mayhem reigned all the way from the airport to an enormous square downtown with an imposing mosque. One million Muslims knelt there on Friday mornings. Near the mosque was the small Christian church!

Its Christians were upbeat. "God is good to us. Because of all the chaos and confusion we are almost ignored. We can even print Bibles!"

Also printed in the native Farsi language was *God's Smuggler*! The more Andrew learned, the more amazed he became. Iran's Christians were allowed to hold services. They could share their message with all who came to listen. But they were forbidden to go out and evangelize. Yet they were as optimistic as any believers Andrew had met.

"We consider Khomeini a blessing," they insisted of the religious maniac who ruled Iran, "because he is such an obvious tyrant. His intolerance and oppressive use of the police have exposed him as a hypocritical fraud. This 'holy man' of the Muslim faith has soured many Muslims on their religion."

For years Andrew had hesitated to take on Muslim countries. Yet here in the chaos of Iran was a true Suffering Church. He left Iran determined to begin his ministry to Muslim countries, as well as support the ministries already there. He also set up prayer groups and began to funnel in assistance to ministries and to individual families who were persecuted.

In 1985 one of the Iranian pastors, Mehdi Dibaj, was imprisoned. He became an inspiration for Christians not yet in prison. For two years Mehdi was confined to a black hole only one square meter in size. But in his confinement he grew so near God he protested being moved into a regular cell.

After one of Andrew's 1985 trips into the Muslim world, he prayed for direction. What should he do that he was not doing to keep Open Doors a viable instrument for spreading the Gospel and supporting the Suffering Church? Open Doors had expanded into nearly twenty offices all over the world. But its many activities overwhelmed Andrew, especially since he wanted to focus his own efforts on the Muslim world. After much prayer the answer came. He must do less management and Johan must do more. The truth was that Andrew was only a mediocre manager, whereas Johan was an exceptional one. So Andrew convinced the board of directors of Open Doors to name Johan Executive Vice President.

At age fifty-eight Andrew felt great relief. Why had he waited so long? Apparently it was God's will. He couldn't help thinking of *Building in a Broken World,* the book he wrote in 1980 based on the life of Nehemiah. The Bible only hinted at all those who must have helped Nehemiah rebuild the wall around Jerusalem. And yet on reflection, anyone reading the story of Nehemiah had to realize many helped him. Only a team, an organization, could have accomplished such a feat. Likewise, Andrew had always felt all the Open Doors people worked side by side. Yet somehow he had not realized until 1985 that it was Johan who should be directing Open Doors.

Even though Andrew was no longer "in charge," he continued to have uncanny "insights." Most believed the Cold War between the European Communist countries and the western democracies was a permanent problem. The Russian leader Brezhnev had died in 1982, only to be followed by the hard-liners Andropov and Chernenko. Few expected relations with the western democracies to improve. Yet Andrew truly sensed the end of Communism in Russia. Because he believed to the very depths of his soul in the power of prayer, he sanctioned a worldwide prayer chain, using every Open Doors office and thousands of friends and supporters. He vowed his "Seven Years of Prayer for the Soviet Union" would run from 1984 to 1990. "Prayers will fly up to God twenty-four hours a day, seven days a week!" he declared.

How the face of Russia and all of Communism changed during those years! By 1985 Gorbachev was the leader of Russia. Within one year he had introduced the concepts of perestroika, which meant rebuilding, and glasnost, a new openness. And his program seemed to be sincere and not just a ruse. The time seemed ripe for Open Doors to do something major. In 1987 during prayer Andrew pleaded with God for a plan. Then while praying he had a vision: truckloads of Bibles were rolling into Russia! When border guards tried to stop them, the truckers had cried, "We come in the name of Jesus—you cannot stop us!"[1]

Andrew believed his vision forecast things to come very soon, even though most of his coworkers thought he was crazy. But that same year brought concrete evidence the end of Russian Communism was near. A prominent

Dutchman began arranging a human rights conference between Russia and the western democracies. Publicity would be minimal. The tone of the meeting was to be nonconfrontational. The Dutchman asked Andrew, a champion of nonconfrontational meetings, to help with the planning in an unofficial capacity. Andrew was astonished to learn the Russians had initiated the idea of the conference. "The Russians want a conference to discuss present and upcoming problems," explained the Dutchman.

Upcoming problems? Were Russian leaders anticipating the breakdown of Communism in Russia? The more Andrew heard, the more astonished he became. He was stunned to hear that the Dutchman wanted him to represent Holland at the conference. Was Andrew so respected now? Perhaps *God's Smuggler* was the reason. Quietly, as far as Andrew was concerned, the book had become almost a Christian classic and had been translated into thirty languages. More than ten million copies, a staggering figure, had been sold all over the world. But most importantly to Andrew, copies of the book were found, legally or otherwise, in every Communist country and every Muslim country.

"I had misgivings about publishing my story," reflected Andrew, "but God knew better."

Soon he, a Bible smuggler not able to cross their borders since the publication of *God's Smuggler* in 1967, was meeting Russian officials in Holland to plan the conference. Once again Johan Companjen showed how invaluable he was to Andrew's organization. Johan and another coworker made a presentation to the Russians before the conference that was very well received. This "Conference

181

on Human Rights and International Cooperation" was held January 1988 in the Dutch province of Zeeland. Many distinguished people and religious leaders attended, including Rosalynn Carter, wife of former American President Jimmy Carter.

At one dinner Andrew was startled to hear a Russian lament, "If only we could return to the pure faith of men like Moses and Jesus."

During the conference Andrew had been having recurring thoughts that he could no longer dismiss. Why not strike now? Why not offer the Russians one million Bibles? The year 1988 was deemed the one thousandth anniversary of the Russian Orthodox Church. Why not offer the Bibles to the Russian Orthodox Church? Back in 1967 a Russian Orthodox priest had asked Andrew, "Why do you give your Bibles only to the Protestants? We need Scriptures, too." Maybe over twenty years later Andrew could answer that earnest priest, who had been perfectly right in his complaint.

Later in the conference Andrew stood up to speak. A very experienced speaker, he softened up his listeners with a true anecdote about Angola. In Angola he had suggested to a Communist guerilla leader that they at least compare the Bible to the "wisdom" of Marx. He offered Bibles to the leader and all his immediate henchmen. The Communist leader had surprised him by agreeing to Andrew's proposal.

"You see, no people can be happy if they are forced to accept one certain system," concluded Andrew as he finished his anecdote. "It means something to them only if they choose it themselves." Then Andrew dropped the hammer. "The same is true for the Russian people. As a beginning, therefore, I am offering one million Bibles as a gift to the Russian Orthodox Church."

A Communist official from Poland challenged him after the speech. "What if I came into your offices and wanted to give each of your workers a copy of Marx? Would you let me?"

The idea repulsed Andrew, but he realized there was only one answer. "By all means."

The official shook his hand. "Then we are friends."

Andrew was amazed by the warm response from the Communists. "I have a Bible at home," said one Russian, "and it's a very important cultural book."

Another joked, "You won't dump all one million on us in one night like you did in China, will you?"

But were these Russians merely skillful diplomats? When the conference ended, Andrew still had no official response to his offer. Next he wrote Patriarch Pimen, the spiritual leader of the entire Russian Orthodox Church, to extend his offer officially. The Bible he offered was the New Testament with the Psalms. For several months he received no response at all. Then in July 1988 he received a reply from a Russian Orthodox official that included this beautiful line:

> "We would like to thank you sincerely for this lavish expression of Christian love and consider it a pleasant duty to inform you that we have agreed to accept the edition of the Holy Scriptures offered to us."[2]

When Andrew remembered his vision of truckloads of

Bibles rolling into Russia, he was shaken. It had been just one year since he had that vision during prayer. In January 1989 Andrew made his first trip to Russia in twenty-two years. The Human Rights conference was convening again. It was obvious Russia had changed. Far fewer soldiers were visible on the streets. Vendors sold merchandise on the sidewalks. Musicians performed on street corners. People were smiling, not staring gloomily at their feet. During the conference Andrew presented the first shipment of one hundred thousand Bibles to the Russian Orthodox church in a ceremony at the Danilov Monastery. The church had endured over seventy years of suppression.

Andrew praised the Russians. "You showed the western countries your faith, your love, and your endurance."

But then Father Vitali Borovoi floored Andrew. "The gift of these Bibles is given by Open Doors and Brother Andrew. How symbolic that is. According to tradition, the Apostle Andrew was the first to preach the Gospel of our Lord in Russia. You, Brother Andrew, continue that apostleship."

To be compared to one of the apostles! Would anyone ever doubt again Brother Andrew's calling and the purpose of Open Doors? He was as elated as his recipients as he personally distributed some of the Bibles. Typical of the generosity of people in religious life, one monk whispered to Andrew that he should distribute Bibles to the lay people, too. He must not give Bibles just to church officials and clerics. Of course, Andrew knew that was true.

Russia continued to change in spite of old Communist hard-liners trying to stop Gorbachev's efforts. In the spring of 1989 Gorbachev was able to push through free elections! Communism was repudiated by the Russian people.

The whole scenario in Russia was beyond belief to most people. Since 1917 freedom in Russia had been thought to be dead. Since World War II freedom in the Eastern European countries had been thought to be dead. But freedom was not dead. "Only dormant," marveled Andrew.

Everywhere in the world Communism was disintegrating or at least easing up. The massacre of students in Tiananmen Square by Red Chinese soldiers in June 1989 seemed the exception. But Andrew and others who worked closely with Communists knew only too well the students had pushed too far, too fast. The students, in turn, had been goaded into extreme recklessness by American television reporters. The incident in every way was not in harmony with the nonconfrontational, low-profile meetings that swayed Communists. If Andrew had confronted Russian soldiers in Red Square, what would have happened?

Meanwhile Communism in Europe was in its death throes. The Iron Curtain's most oppressive symbol, the Berlin Wall, was attacked spontaneously by East Germans on November 9, 1989. And the authorities did nothing! Christians marched into East Berlin with a banner that blazed words from Psalm 24:7: "Lift up your heads, O you gates. . .that the King of glory may come in." Inside East Berlin Christians openly evangelized for the first time in over forty years! Communism in East Germany was dying, judged by its citizens a colossal failure. It was astonishing to anyone familiar with the rigidity of the old-time, hard-line Communists. But the Berlin Wall came down, and its collapse was followed by one Communist government after another.

In 1990 Andrew was allowed to present the last of the

one million Bibles to the patriarch of the Russian Orthodox Church. Later, he was thrilled to hear Joseph Bondarenko, know as the "Billy Graham of Russia," preach in Red Square. Bondarenko had been imprisoned many years but now he not only preached in freedom, but handed out New Testaments to all those who wanted the precious Word of God!

Andrew couldn't help saying to Bondarenko later, "You know Open Doors prayed seven years for Russia."

"Don't stop! We had to pray for seventy years!"

Even the worst of all European Communist countries, Albania, loosened its grip. Hoxha, the tyrant, had died in 1985. In 1990 its citizens rose as a force against Communism. But its disintegration, as in some other Communist countries, was ugly. The country was in chaos and crime was rampant as Open Doors went in with other mission groups in 1991. The shaky government urged them to come, as if they were willing to try anything to quell the riotous atmosphere. The evangelists were given a huge stadium in the capital of Tirana for their pulpit. "Albania needs spiritual help," said the minister of culture hopefully.

Andrew was one of the first to preach to the crowds, which totaled only eight thousand over five days. Crowds were small because many Albanians remained suspicious. After all, the tyrant Hoxha had declared that belief in God must ripped out by the roots! However, now Albanian state television telecast the first service to the entire country. Newspapers covered the entire revival. Andrew was delighted. So what if they weren't getting huge crowds yet? Only a few years before no preacher could even enter the country. They made 157 converts during the week—and they distributed ten thousand copies of the Book of John and seven thousand New Testaments.

Some Albanians begged Andrew to bring them Bibles translated into modern Albanian. As Andrew had discovered many years earlier, no Bibles existed in their native Albanian tongues. Christians used a Bible that was either in Latin or in Greek. Andrew found the innocence of the Albanians wonderful. "We will have a party for the first Bible you bring," they wrote him. "Please bring Coca-Cola and cheese and crackers."

What a change from the ruthless Hoxha!

Andrew was obliged to satisfy the Albanians. By 1993 he had a complete translation printed in a modern Albanian language. And he did not forget to bring Coca-Cola and cheese and crackers to Tirana. At the party were two hundred officials and clerics. Catholics, Orthodox, Protestants, and the nonreligious alike gushed over the new Albanian Bible.

One politician declared,

"The past fifty years, the devil reigned in our country. Now that we have the Bible, we hope the devil will be expelled."[3]

Albania was not only once a Communist country, but also once predominantly Muslim. This event seemed to bridge Andrew's many years of efforts in the Communist countries and his budding efforts in the Muslim countries.

Now, more and more, Andrew was focused on the Muslim world.

fourteen

To further his Muslim efforts Andrew hosted a retreat in 1991 for twelve Iranian pastors and their wives. They prayed together, studied Scripture, and swapped stories. The pastors walked on the beach with their wives. They returned to Iran refreshed but well-burdened with Bibles and Christian materials.

Conditions in Iran, however, worsened for Christian churches shortly after that retreat. The Iran government ruthlessly suppressed Christianity and arrests were made. Many of the pastors left Iran. One pastor who stayed was Haik Hovsepian. Haik spoke out for the release from prison of Pastor Mehdi Dibaj. He told Andrew, "When the authorities kill me, it will be for speaking out, not for being silent."

Andrew doubted Haik's protest was a virtual death sentence. But by 1994 it was obvious that conditions for Christians in the Muslim world were getting worse all the time. After nine years in jail, Mehdi Dibaj was formally charged with apostasy, or the crime of leaving the Muslim faith. Apostasy was punishable by death. In his defense he declared his love of Christ. He could not return to the Muslim faith because he was already in the arms of God. If they killed him, he would just enter the kingdom that much sooner and be with Christ forever. The court sentenced him to hang.

While Andrew organized prayer chains for Dibaj, Haik was publicly protesting in Iran. Mysteriously, Dibaj was released, but the joy Christians felt over this sudden turn of events was short-lived. A short time later Haik was kidnapped and murdered. At Haik's funeral Mehdi Dibaj declared, "I should have died, not Haik Hovsepian."

A few months later, Mehdi Dibaj was murdered. Then Haik's successor as pastor was murdered. The government denied any involvement, but few doubted who was behind the killings. Iran's Muslim government of the 1990s was the most murderous regime yet. Today Iran is on Brother Andrew's list of the world's ten most brutal regimes to Christians. For some time, Open Doors has monitored every government in the world for religious tolerance, a project known as "World Watch."

By the mid-1990s Andrew came to believe that Muslims were the greatest challenge—if not also the greatest threat—to the church of Christ. Muslims are not only fanatically intolerant but determined to prevail by any means. Christians cannot match their treachery, but the most disheartening thing to Andrew is that Christians have not matched their commitment either, even though the Bible calls Christians to that level of commitment. Andrew was so deeply concerned that he decided to devote his own personal ministry to two efforts:

1. He would go to the Muslims in the name of Jesus.
2. He would strengthen the Suffering Church already there in the Muslim world.

The Muslim world presented an enormous challenge. It was much more resistant to Christianity than the Communist governments had been. In the Communist countries there had always been a network of believers. In the Muslim world there was rarely a network but only secret and very isolated patches of believers. Yet Andrew pointed out that one of the earliest prayers in the Bible was Abraham's prayer to God for Ishmael, the root of the Arabic peoples (Genesis 17:18): "If only Ishmael might live before thee!" In 1991 Open Doors declared ten years of prayer for the Muslim world.

Andrew also emphasized the need for Christians to reach out to the Muslims with love and not hate. Regarding them as enemies only increased hostilities; regarding them as enemies was certainly not Christ's way. Another mistake was to condemn all of them because of the activities of their most radical groups. Once, on a talk show, the host became exasperated with Andrew's Christian approach.

"What! If those Muslims aren't our enemies, then who is?" cried the host.

"The devil is our enemy," explained Andrew. "Never people."

Andrew also cautioned against making political judgments of conflicts among the Muslim countries. Their histories were old and complex and often intertwined with the maneuverings and intrigues of America and the European countries. Andrew was as dismayed as anyone that the mass killer Idi Amin, after he was overthrown in Uganda in 1979, was given sanctuary in the Muslim countries. But Andrew had to put that injustice behind him, consoling himself that God would judge Amin. For the sake of the Suffering Church, Andrew had dealt with many killers.

He had even talked to Muslim terrorists like Yassir Arafat, the leader of the Palestinians. Like so many political situations Andrew had encountered, the Palestinian-Israeli question was very complicated. Although the Palestinians were often characterized by their most radical Muslim terrorist groups, Andrew met Christians among them. These Christians were isolated and condemned on all sides for all kinds of reasons. The truth was that most of the Christians within the borders of Israel were Palestinians. "In the Palestinian town of Gaza there is a small Baptist church as well as a mission hospital," someone pointed out.

As Andrew focused more and more on the Muslim countries, he realized how the percentage of Christians living there had plummeted during the twentieth century. Christians in Syria and Iraq were decimated, dropping from between thirty and forty percent of the population to three and four percent! During the same time the percentages in Palestine and Jordan fell from thirty-two to four percent. Andrew felt as he had so many years before in the Communist countries: He must strengthen the small Christian church that remained!

Andrew had visited many Muslims in the Middle East countries around Israel. But the Muslim world stretched far beyond those countries. It was important to realize that like the old Communist world, the Muslim world was not monolithic. To the south in the vast countries of Africa were tens of millions of Christians in Muslim countries. Some were tolerated, some were not. To the east were extremely oppressive Muslim countries like Afghanistan and Pakistan, as well as more permissive ones like sprawling Indonesia, formerly the Dutch East Indies. "Indonesia has over thirteen million Christians," observed Andrew.

By 1995, although Andrew was completely focused on the Muslim world, Open Doors still maintained a global view. Open Doors itself was forty years old, and Andrew was now sixty-seven. In spite of his perilous life, he had already lived longer than both his parents. Papa had not reached sixty, and poor Mama had not lived to see fifty. It was no wonder people began to ask about his successor. Some Christian ministries had disintegrated after their founders died. But there was no mystery about Andrew's successor. It was a simply a matter of formalizing the succession.

"Johan Companjen is the new President of Open Doors International," announced the board of directors, to the surprise of no one. Andrew became President Emeritus, but the title meant nothing to him. Johan had been running Open Doors International for some time anyway. Unlike Johan, Andrew had neither the knowledge nor the desire to travel around with a lap-top computer. And unlike Johan, Andrew had neither the knowledge nor the desire to design a website for the Internet. Fortunately, both men agreed completely on the aims of the Open Doors organization. Open Doors International of the 1990s formalized a threefold strategy:

1. Deliver Bibles—by whatever means possible— into countries where they are banned or restricted.
2. Train church leaders who live in countries opposed to the Gospel.
3. Support and encourage individual believers who are suffering for their faith.

On May 12, 1997, Brother Andrew's sixty-ninth birthday, the World Evangelical Fellowship honored him with its Religious Liberty Award in front of six thousand people at Rotary Stadium in Abbotsford, British Columbia. It was humbling for Brother Andrew, who had usually kept such a low profile. His exploits in assisting persecuted Christians were deemed legendary. He was glad only when he heard the speaker admit there were also many unsung heroes.

Brother Andrew responded to his tribute by emphasizing the continuing need for forgiveness and reconciliation toward the persecutors. The battle was really with the devil, he insisted. He urged Christians not only to pray for the Suffering Church, but to complain to their own governments about persecution against Christians in other countries. At a press conference later he emphasized the need for Christian leaders to remain in these countries of persecution, much as he had urged the East Germans many years before. The battle was there. And God had strategically put them there.

Today Open Doors International has major offices in seventeen countries around the world. In Asia and the Pacific their offices are in the Philippines, Malaysia, New Zealand, Australia, and Korea. In the Western Hemisphere, the offices are in Brazil, the United States, and Canada. The one office in Africa is still located in South Africa. The other eight offices are in Europe: Holland, the United Kingdom, Italy, Spain, Norway, Switzerland, France, and Denmark. Open Doors has always been run by a phenomenally lean staff. Only about two hundred workers man all the offices.

The organization as a whole maintains work on five fronts they have dubbed "battle zones." These battle zones include forty-five countries. One battle zone remains the old Communist bloc countries of Eastern Europe. This is a critical area now to nourish. Andrew has been disturbed at how little help western countries have offered while these countries struggle to adopt capitalistic economies. It is not inconceivable that some of these countries could slip back to Communism if life does not improve for their citizens. In the list of over one hundred countries Andrew's World Watch graded according to their degree of religious freedom, the only abusive former Eastern European Communist regimes are small, and now independent, states that are dominantly Muslim. Russia, once the most terrifying ogre in the world to westerners, is midway on the list, as tolerant to religion as Greece!

In the battle zones there are hundreds of individual "soldiers" crying out for help. Many have become specific targets of persecutors, both official and unofficial. Often a local judge or law enforcement officer takes it upon himself to persecute Christians. Too frequently, vigilantes have persecuted Christians.

In the northern Caucasus area of the old Communist Soviet Union the Baptist pastor Alexei Sitnikov was kidnapped in 1998. One month later an American missionary, Herb Gregg, was kidnapped nearby. No demands were made by these kidnappers, leading many to assume the two had been murdered. Sitnikov's replacement, Aleksandr Kulakov, disappeared in March 1999. Three Orthodox priests have also disappeared. In mid-1999 a woman claimed to have seen Kulakov's severed head on display! These depressing facts only make Open Doors more determined to supply religious material to this old battle zone. A massive effort, called Project Samuel, has been underway in Russia to deliver one million children's Bibles.

A second battle zone is Latin America. This war for souls is primarily in Cuba but is also in some Latin countries that have persecuted Protestants. Open Doors is committed to providing over three hundred thousand Bibles and other Christian materials to these countries. Also they seek to train three thousand ministers a year. Other activities, as always, include visiting prisoners as well as helping widows and orphans. In general the future of the Suffering Church in Latin America looks bright. But individuals still suffer greatly there. Peru, particularly, is intolerant of Protestants, officially and unofficially. Romulo Saune, a Quechua pastor, was murdered in 1992 by Communist guerrillas. Another noted case was the five-year imprisonment of Wuillie Ruiz under false charges.

Cuba remains the worst. After the pope's visit in January 1998 Castro wanted the world to think he had mellowed.

But in 1998 Pastor Nieto's sister was murdered. And in 1999 Cuban soldiers confiscated and burned thousands of "subversive" Bibles. The war goes on!

A third battle zone is Africa south of the Sahara Desert. This is a much more difficult battle than in Latin America. Many tens of millions of Christians are in jeopardy, as much from civil wars as from Muslim oppression. Bibles are important to strengthen the Suffering Church, but much of Open Doors' emphasis is on training pastors. After all, the literacy rate for Africa is very low. Many Africans cannot read any book, let alone the Bible. So the goals are to train two thousand pastors annually and distribute 120,000 Bibles.

Individual "soldiers" suffer there, too. In Nigeria, ironically once thought to be one of the most promising areas, Christians have been besieged by Muslim vigilantes. Dozens of churches were burned in the late 1990s. Worshipers were attacked by machete-hacking Muslims during a church service. Shops of Christians were pillaged. And the authorities looked the other way. "Who can catch spirits?" they were quoted as saying as they laughed.

A fourth battle zone is Asia. Like Africa, many tens of millions of Christians are already there. The key countries are Red China and Vietnam, and goals are high. In both adult and children's versions Open Doors aims to provide two million Bibles. Pastors have to be trained at the rate of five thousand per year. The church is still severely persecuted in many Asian countries. In the list of over one hundred countries World Watch graded according to their degree of religious freedom, four of the ten worst are Asian countries. It was small consolation that only tens of thousands of Christians live in two of the four, North Korea and

Laos. About seventy million live in the other two: Red China and Vietnam.

In Vietnam, Pastor Peter was imprisoned from 1996 to 1998 for preaching the Gospel to rural tribes. His children were denied schooling. In China, Cheng Meiying, a woman pastor of a house church, was so savagely beaten by police that she suffered blackouts months later. Hundreds of Christians were in prison in China because preaching carries a mandatory three-year sentence. Much damage has been done unofficially, too. It is common practice to spread vicious gossip about Christians, and gossipers often lie about their promiscuity and love of money. Later, itinerant preachers are at a loss to discover why no Chinese villager will talk to them.

In spite of Andrew's intense interest in all the battle zones, he feels his calling for the twenty-first century is still the Muslim world, the fifth battle zone.

fifteen

Most Muslim people are receptive to the Bible, revering Abraham, Moses, David, and Jesus as holy prophets. But the Muslim governments are ruthlessly intolerant. Officially or unofficially, they have persecuted believers and murdered evangelists. In the list of over one hundred countries World Watch graded according to their degree of religious freedom, the worst persecutors are concentrated in the Muslim world. The four very worst all border the Red Sea: Saudi Arabia, the Sudan, Somalia, and Yemen. Excluding the four Asian countries—Red China, Vietnam, North Korea, and Laos—every one of the thirty worst countries is Muslim!

It is no wonder that Andrew is attracted to this battle zone. But each battle zone has its own needs. In Andrew's opinion, pastors to spread the Gospel and shepherd converts are needed more in this fifth zone than in any other battle zone. With that goal in focus, Open Doors aims to train twenty thousand pastors a year for mission work in the Muslim countries. Although the literacy rate is low in this battle zone, Open Doors still plans to distribute two hundred thousand Bibles. "Of course since 1991 the Muslim world has also been the subject of our ten-year prayer campaign," Andrew adds.

The stories of persecuted individuals in the Muslim world are almost too numerous to count. Andrew knew personally Haik Hovsepian and Mehdi Dibaj, the two pastors murdered in Iran. But other injustices abound, from west to east all across the Muslim world. The sad truth is that radical Muslims are becoming stronger and stronger in the governments. In El-Kosheh, Egypt, one thousand Christians in 1998 were arrested, whipped, kicked, and slugged by local police supposedly investigating a murder. As a result, two Christians died. In 1998 Morocco banned all Bibles. Prior to that, Bibles in foreign languages were legal. In Iran preacher Mohammed Yusefi was murdered in 1996 and his widow and children were persecuted. The fiercely pro-Muslim government of Afghanistan has ruthlessly deported anyone thought to be doing Christian work. All over Indonesia since 1996 Muslims have attacked churches and burned them. On one Sunday alone in 1998, seven churches were destroyed in Jakarta. Topping that was the destruction of eleven churches in the town of Surbaya on a Sunday in 1996. The destruction was not without killings. In Pakistan, Ayub Masih was imprisoned in 1996 for "insulting the prophet Mohammed." This was a sure-fire ploy throughout the Muslim world to get any Christian thrown in prison. A Pakastani named Anwar was imprisoned for five years for defending himself. All his attacker had to say was that Anwar had insulted Mohammed.

And then there are Saudi Arabia and Sudan, the two worst persecutors in the world! The Saudis are surely worse than the worst of the old hard-line Communists. They permit no devotion outside Islam by anyone. Period. If a Christian foreigner is even suspected of praying in private, the authorities will coerce his company into sending him permanently out of the country. Any open devotion is punishable by death. Often Christians serving sentences in prison remain there even after their sentences run out. "To think I once handed out Bibles in a bazaar there," reflected Andrew of his younger days.

Sudan has been deemed the second worst persecutor, but in many ways it is the worst because over two million Christians have suffered there. Everything about the Sudan seems shrouded in confusion or mystery. How many people know it is the largest country in Africa? The southern region is noted for green forests, open savannahs, and waterfalls. Legendary African wildlife live there: lions, elephants, rhinoceros, zebras, giraffes, and dozens of other kinds of exotic animals. And it has a large Christian population. But it is no paradise.

Relief worker Dan Eiffe, a former Catholic priest, has been in South Africa many years. "The suffering in South Africa at its worst, under the worst years of apartheid, is a tea party in comparison with the suffering of the South Sudanese that has been going on so long," he said in an interview broadcast November 26, 1998, on the "700 Club."

By 1999 the civil war between north and south had gone on for sixteen years! The South Sudanese—

Christians, pagans, and even some Muslims—have been starved, bombed, raped, tortured, and murdered by North Sudanese Muslims. Northern Muslims are so ruthless they have repeatedly bombed a hospital in the town of Yei. When food was shipped into a starving village, Muslim soldiers attacked and set the food supplies on fire. In another village they deliberately destroyed all the medical supplies. United Nations security officials have attested that North Sudan bombed or attacked humanitarian projects in South Sudan more than forty times in 1998 alone! Two Catholic priests who were arrested by the North Sudanese in 1998 were charged with terrorist activity and tortured.

As an added outrage, Christian have been captured by the Muslims only to be put into slavery. If captured and healthy, they are taken north as slaves. Girls are often used as prostitutes, and boys have often been abused in the same way. The proof of this practice has been confirmed many times over by Christians who have been "bought back." Some agencies have done just that. Christian Solidarity International has redeemed more than four thousand Sudanese slaves from 1996 to 1998.

As the twenty-first century arrives, it is little wonder that Brother Andrew continues to persevere for the Suffering Church in the Muslim world. He has come a long way from clumsily smuggling a few religious tracts into Poland in 1955. Now his Open Doors organization strengthens the Suffering Church in forty-five countries. But the battle against the devil is far from over. . .

Bibliography

I. Books by Brother Andrew (or as told by Brother Andrew):

Andrew, Brother. *Building in a Broken World.* Wheaton, Illinois: Tyndale House Publishers, 1981.

Andrew, Brother with Verne Becker. *For the Love of My Brothers.* Minneapolis: Bethany House Publishers, 1998.

Andrew, Brother with Susan Devore Williams. *And God Changed His Mind.* Old Tappan, NJ: Chosen Books (Fleming H. Revell Company), 1990.

Sherrill, John, and Elizabeth Sherrill with Brother Andrew. *God's Smuggler.* New York: New American Library, 1967.

Wooding, Dan with Brother Andrew. *Brother Andrew.* Minneapolis: Bethany House Publishers, 1983.

II. Other books of interest:

Chambers, Oswald. *My Utmost for His Highest.* New York: Dodd, Mead & Company, 1935.

Fischer, Louis. *The Story of Indonesia.* New York: Harper & Brothers, 1959.

Moyer, Elgin, ed. revised by Earle E. Cairns, ed. *Wycliffe Biographical Dictionary of the Church.* Chicago: Moody Press, 1982.

Ten Boom, Corrie with Buckingham, Jamie. *Tramp for the Lord.* Old Tappan, NJ: Fleming H. Revell Company, 1974.

Ward, Charles G., ed. *The Billy Graham Christian Worker's Handbook.* Minneapolis: World Wide Publications, 1993.

Woodbridge, John D., ed. *Ambassadors for Christ.* Chicago: Moody Press, 1994.

Endnotes

Chapter 5

1. Moyer, Elgin (ed.), revised by Earl E. Cairns. *Wycliffe Biographical Dictionary of the Church.* Chicago: Moody Press, 1982. Used with permission.

Chapter 6

1. Chambers, Oswald. *My Utmost for His Highest.* New York: Dodd, Mead & Company, 1935. November 5 entry. Used with permission.
2. Andrew, Brother, with Vern Becker. *For the Love of My Brothers.* Minneapolis: Bethany House Publishers, 1998, p. 30. Used with permission.
3. Wooding, Dan, with Brother Andrew. *Brother Andrew.* Minneapolis: Bethany House Publishers, 1983, p. 57. Used with permission.

Chapter 8

1. Wooding, p. 71.

Chapter 12

1. Andrew, p. 73
2. Ibid.
3. Andrew, p. 99.
4. Andrew, p. 98.
5. Andrew, p. 121.
6. Andrew, p. 132

Chapter 13

1. Andrew, p. 157.
2. Andrew, p. 171.
3. Andrew, p. 194.

HEROES OF THE FAITH

This exciting biographical series explores the lives of famous Christian men and women throughout the ages. These trade paper books will inspire and encourage you to follow the example of these "Heroes of the Faith" who made Christ the center of their existence. 208 pages each. Only $3.97 each!

Available wherever books are sold.
Or order from:
Barbour Publishing, Inc.
P.O. Box 719
Uhrichsville, Ohio 44683
http://www.barbourbooks.com

If you order by mail, add $2.00 to your order for shipping.
Prices subject to change without notice.